CRITICAL ACCLAIM FOR THE WORK OF SUSAN REIGLER

"Susan Reigler explores not only Bourbon but takes you inside several relatively unknown destinations." **—WHISKY ADVOCATE**

"This is a very good book for any Bourbon lover's bar library." **—BOURBONENTHUSIAST.COM**

"This is a very well-designed book with many excellent color photographs that will look good on any coffee table, but it will probably not rest there very long. It is filled with valuable information that will have you picking it up every time you want to entertain guests. . . . You will find yourself referencing this book often as the book supplies a wealth of useful information." **—BOURBONVEACH.COM**

"One of the most detailed and comprehensive guides . . . a lifeline for anyone looking for a unique experience." **—SEATTLE BOOK REVIEW**

"This book is a wonderful reference." **—BLOOMSBURY REVIEW**

"Bourbon lovers will find a vacation in a binding with this wonderful book . . . as well as the glorious art." **—LOUISVILLE COURIER-JOURNAL**

"In a reader-friendly format . . . everyone, from the Bourbon connoisseur to the amateur enthusiast, can appreciate this how-to guide, which embraces the rich heritage and sophistication of a true Kentucky classic." **—KENTUCKY POST**

"The information here has more than enough detail to assist in planning an outing for the day or a weekend getaway. From the pictures to the narratives, Kentuckians may be more tempted than ever to never leave the state." **—BOWLING GREEN DAILY NEWS**

"The bold taste of Bourbon can now be enjoyed by newcomers looking to experiment with the rich flavors of this uniquely American beverage." **—NOVUS VINUM**

"Very approachable and easy to read." **—LIFE CURRENTS**

"Beautifully presented." **—TRAVEL DISTILLED**

"Deeply researched and thoroughly indexed, this guide should satisfy any thirsty and curious visitor to the Bluegrass State." **—PUBLISHERS WEEKLY**

Kentucky Bourbon

Kentucky Bourbon

The Essential Guide to the American Spirit

SUSAN REIGLER

FOREWORD BY JULIAN VAN WINKLE III

Countryman Press

An Imprint of W. W. Norton & Company
Independent Publishers Since 1923

For information about permission to reproduce selections from this book, write to
Permissions, Countryman Press, 500 Fifth Avenue, New York, NY 10110

For information about special discounts for bulk purchases, please contact
W. W. Norton Special Sales at specialsales@wwnorton.com or 800-233-4830

Manufacturing by Toppan Leefung
Book design by Chrissy Kurpeski
Maps by Michael Borop (sitesatlas.com)
Production manager: Devon Zahn

Countryman Press
www.countrymanpress.com

An imprint of W. W. Norton & Company, Inc.
500 Fifth Avenue, New York, NY 10110
www.wwnorton.com

978-1-68268-875-5

1 2 3 4 5 6 7 8 9 0

For Joanna

1. Buffalo Trace Distillery
2. Old Forester Distilling Company
3. Green River Distilling Company
4. Four Roses Distillery
5. Wild Turkey Distilling Company
6. James B. Beam Distilling Company
7. Heaven Hill Distillery
8. Stitzel-Weller Distillery
9. Willett Distillery
10. Maker's Mark Distillery

11. Bulleit Distilling Company
12. Woodford Reserve Distillery
13. Kentucky Artisan Distillery
14. Michter's Distillery
15. Barrel House Distilling Company
16. James E. Pepper Distilling Company
17. MB Roland Distillery
18. Louisville Distilling Company
19. Limestone Branch Distillery
20. Bluegrass Distillers

21. Old Pogue Distillery
22. Rabbit Hole Distillery
23. Town Branch Distillery
24. Kentucky Peerless Distilling Company
25. Wilderness Trail
26. Casey Jones Distillery
27. Castle & Key Distillery
28. Dueling Grounds Distillery
29. Second Sight Spirits
30. New Riff Distilling

31. Boone County Distilling Company
32. Neeley Family Distillery
33. Bardstown Bourbon Company
34. Jeptha Creed Distillery
35. Augusta Distillery
36. Lux Row Distillers
37. Preservation Distillery
38. Log Still Distillery

CONTENTS

FOREWORD

If you don't already know of Susan Reigler, let me introduce her. I first remember seeing Susan's name when she worked as the restaurant critic for the *Louisville Courier-Journal* in 1992. I wouldn't attempt to dine at a restaurant unless I first checked with Susan's spot-on recommendations.

Her transition, around 2005, from food critic to author and Bourbon expert was marked by her ability to tell compelling stories about the industry and its key players. Her experience in critiquing restaurants and beverages honed her skills in tasting and evaluating spirits, which became a central theme in her later works, which included books on Bourbon. This background also facilitated her involvement in whiskey festivals and her leadership roles, such as being president of the Bourbon Women Association, further solidifying her status as an authority in the field. Her expertise is also recognized through her role as a Bourbon columnist for *Food & Dining*, *Covey Rise*, and *Bourbon+* magazines.

A biologist and former biology professor, Susan brings a unique scientific lens to her Bourbon analyses. She has a deep understanding of the chemical and biological processes involved in Bourbon production. This wisdom allows her to provide insightful commentary on topics such as yeast strains, grain sources, and the effects of charred oak barrels on the spirit. My grandfather Pappy was known for not being a fan of scientists hanging around his distillery, but when zeroing in on particular flavor profiles from the mash fermentation to barrel aging, experts can be very helpful to distillers.

The story of Bourbon is personal to me, and it's woven into the very fabric of who I am. My family's name has been synonymous with this industry for generations, and I feel a deep sense of responsibility to carry forward our legacy. It's humbling to reflect on my family's journey, from a time when we were among only a handful of small, independent producers fighting to keep the craft alive to now, when the world looks to Kentucky for its most exceptional spirits. My role in this industry has been to honor the past while striving to preserve the authenticity and soul of what Bourbon is. The Van Winkle brand has always been about quality over quantity, patience over speed, and an uncompromising dedication to creating something worthy of the history behind it. I see this philosophy echoed in Susan's work, and it's why her contributions to the industry are so vital.

When I first read through Susan's manuscript for this book, I assumed that it would be a description of several Kentucky distilleries and the whiskeys that they produce. But she dug deep into the original careers of these distillery owners and how they branched out from their starting careers and ended up in the distilling business. I love connecting the dots among distilleries, which is bound to happen in this industry, and we see instances of the camaraderie and support among the players. I, for one, wouldn't be here without the help and support of Jimmy Russell at Wild Turkey, Andrea Wilson while she was at Stitzel-Weller, Mark Brown at Buffalo Trace, and many others in the industry.

Reading this book will introduce you to the pioneers and newcomers alike. From the iconic Buffalo Trace to the more recent arrivals such as Bardstown Bourbon Company, rich descriptions of distillery histories and their geographical locations will give you an immediate sense of place and terroir. Yes, "terroir" is a French word, but think back to the historically French beginning of the word "Bourbon" found in Susan's introduction. How fortunate for whiskey aficionados and novices alike to have the benefit of Susan Riegler's knowledge and research that has resulted in this guide to the spirit.

There is so much interesting historical information in this book, much of which I was unaware. Did you know that the popularity of Bourbon in New Orleans was driven by newly arrived French royalists in the early 1880s? They were starved for their beloved, barrel-aged Cognac, not easily obtainable, so they turned to the beautiful brown liquid from charred oak barrels that made their way from Kentucky down the Ohio and Mississippi rivers. Ever heard of Bourbon Street?

Another random tidbit of Kentucky Bourbon history is in the chapter on the present-day Castle & Key Distillery that Edmund H. Taylor created in 1887. E. H. Taylor, his name a popular brand today, initiated the Bottled-in-Bond Act in 1897, making it America's first federal consumer protection law.

So rich is the Samuels family history, and the story of Marge Samuels giving birth in the 1950s to what we now know was marketing genius. She spurred the growth of one of the most iconic brands on the market today. The rest, as they say, is history, and the Maker's Mark property in Loretto is well-deserving of the name Star Hill. So much is going on there that it requires a dedicated field trip to take it all in.

Along with Marge Samuels, Susan shows us the importance of women in the industry, their roles growing tremendously during the last 30-plus years. Who doesn't love a wonderful success story about a woman accepting an entry-level job, wanting to support her equestrian habit, then rising to master distiller, as is the inspiring case of Elizabeth McCall? Peggy Noe Stevens has been an influential figure in the Bourbon industry for more than 30 years. She founded the Bourbon Women Association and played a crucial role in creating the Kentucky Bourbon Trail. Marianne Eaves was Kentucky's first woman master distiller since Prohibition. Today, women form a huge part of the Bourbon industry, and Susan details their roles very well. She shares the origins of Bourbon tourism, birthed by savvy women in their infinite wisdom, once they recognized that the public indeed was interested in observing the production of their favorite spirit.

Susan is a certified executive Bourbon steward. A significant part of the certification involves developing and testing one's sensory skills, which includes nosing and tasting various Bourbons and identifying different aromas. This task can prove challenging, as it requires the refining of one's palate and sensory perception. Susan has a palate that I can only dream of!

In the end, *Kentucky Bourbon: The Essential Guide to the American Spirit* is more than a celebration of Bourbon; it's a tribute to the people who pour their passion into every barrel. It's a reminder that, while Bourbon may be born in the distillery, its spirit is nurtured by the people who love it. So as you read this book, take your time. Much like a fine Bourbon, it's best enjoyed slowly, with an appreciation for the history, craftsmanship, and people who make it all possible. Once you've read the book, you can tell whether a particular distillery speaks to you, decide whether you want to visit, plan your trip, and chart your path.

I'm honored to write this foreword and to count Susan Reigler as a friend and colleague. Her contributions to Bourbon's story are invaluable, and I can't wait for you to discover all the richness that this book has to offer. My hope is that it will inspire you to visit Kentucky and the wonderful distilleries here and learn about how America's only native spirit, Kentucky Bourbon whiskey, is made.

Take a tour, have a drink, and cheers to Susan Reigler!

Julian Van Winkle III

INTRODUCTION

In prehistoric Gaul, the ancient Celts revered Borvo, a god of healing springs later identified with Apollo. In Gaulish, their language, *boruo* means "hot spring" and fittingly has close etymological ties to "brew" and "boil" in English. Over the centuries, the god's name morphed into the first half of Bourbon l'Archambault, a small town near the geographic center of what has become France.

In 913, King Charles III of France gave control of the chateau in Bourbon l'Archambault to a nobleman named Aymar, making him the first Lord of Bourbon. That title passed through nine generations of male descendants before coming to Mathilde, Lady of Bourbon, who married an aristocrat from Champagne. Their great-great granddaughter, Beatrice of Burgundy, married a son of King Louis IX of France, and their eldest son became the first duke of Bourbon, founding the House of Bourbon as we know it. Ten generations later, Henri IV became the first Bourbon king of France, and he established the first successful French colonies in North America.

In 1776, Henri's fifth-great grandson, King Louis XVI, authorized the shipment of supplies to the Continental Army of the Thirteen Colonies to aid the American War of Independence. During the war, Virginia's government issued the Corn Patch and Cabin Rights Act to encourage settlement of its frontier. The writ offered 400 acres of land to any man who built a cabin and raised a crop of 40 acres of corn, and it allowed him to purchase another 400 acres at $1 per acre. When the colonies became the United States of America, the boundaries of Virginia included what later became Kentucky, most of the Great Lakes states (formally: the Territory Northwest of the River Ohio), and West Virginia, an area too vast to govern effectively from Richmond. As more Europeans poured across the Appalachian Mountains, county and state lines changed. In 1785, officials split a section of Fayette County, Virginia—named for war hero Gilbert du Motier, Marquis de la Fayette—into Bourbon County, Virginia, named for King Louis XVI, which included roughly a quarter of present-day Kentucky. This area eventually became known as Old Bourbon, and in 1792, Kentucky split from Virginia to become the 15th state admitted to the Union.

The story so far involves a lot of places and people but no whiskey. That's because, prior to the Revolutionary War, American colonists primarily drank rum. Massachusetts alone had 60 rum distilleries, which used a steady supply of sugarcane from Caribbean plantations. The British owned those plantations and controlled the sugar trade to America, which naturally ended with the outbreak of the revolution. So American farmer-distillers pivoted to homegrown grain. Rye whiskey grew in popularity, and by 1799, when George Washington died, Mount Vernon's largest source of income came from its commercial rye distillery, the biggest in the country at the time, overseen by James Anderson, a Scottish distiller.

In the fledgling country, cash wasn't circulating widely yet, so surplus grain distilled into whiskey served as a barter currency. As farmer-distillers moved westward, they carried their stills and skills with them. Rye prefers cooler climates, so it doesn't flourish in the humid warmth of Kentucky. But corn does, growing easily and abundantly here. So Kentucky farmers naturally made their whiskey with corn. Any surplus often shipped down the Ohio River for the enjoyment of thirsty, Cognac-deprived French royalists who, after the French Revolution, had fled to New Orleans.

That trip downriver could last many months,

especially if a shipment had to wait for spring rains to raise the water level at the Falls of the Ohio at Louisville. That extra time in wooden casks—heated to bend the staves of the barrel and charred when reused to prevent flavor contamination from prior holdings—gave the whiskey more color and more complex flavors during the voyage. But no one knows for sure when that red Kentucky whiskey became known as Bourbon. Perhaps barrel heads bore a stamp of their contents and origin, something like: Whiskey from (Old) Bourbon County. Perhaps French exiles in New Orleans consumed so much of it on Bourbon Street that it got its name that way—a theory championed more by the denizens of the Crescent City than of the Bluegrass State. Again, no one really knows.

On May 1, 1821, the *Western Citizen* newspaper of Paris, Kentucky, ran an advertisement placed by the Stout & Adams firm of Maysville offering "Bourbon Whiskey," for sale, the first known use of "Bourbon" to mean the beverage. (The same ad listed coffee, pepper, rice, figs, tanners' oil, linseed, ploughs, rope, and more for sale.) As that decade progressed, more companies used the term to describe the whiskey; for example: H. I. de Bruin, also of Maysville, selling "three years old bourbon whisky of superior quality" in 1827.

After the Civil War, farm distilleries all but vanished, replaced by larger commercial enterprises. That state of affairs persisted until Prohibition all but destroyed the distilling industry in 1920. Some Bourbon remained in production outside America, most notably from Waterfill & Frazier in Mexico (page 124). In 1933, Repeal resuscitated the Bourbon business, which, amid the economic devastation of the Great Depression, recovered slowly. In 1939, after the Imperial Japanese Navy attacked Pearl Harbor and America joined World War II, most distilleries in the country converted to making industrial alcohol for the war effort, slowing growth of the spirit once more.

After the war, recovery began yet again, and distilleries developed a newfound eagerness to protect the integrity of the category. (Aging Bourbon under the hot Mexican sun doesn't make for particularly palatable whiskey, it turns out.) With a reminder about how it had helped the war effort, the industry turned to the federal government for help. Few people outside the American whiskey industry were paying attention on May 4, 1964, when President Lyndon Johnson signed into law an Act of Congress declaring Bourbon "a distinctive product of the United States." This statute complemented the Standard of Identity in title 27, part 5.22, of the Code of Federal Regulations, defining the nuts and bolts of Bourbon:

- The mash bill, or ratio of grains, must contain at least 51 percent corn.
- It must distill at no more than 160 proof, or 80 percent alcohol by volume (ABV).
- Only distilled water may dilute the distillate or aged Bourbon to a desired proof.
- It must age in new, charred oak containers.
- It must enter an aging vessel at no more than 125 proof (62.5 percent ABV).
- In the bottle, it must contain a minimum of 80 proof (40 percent ABV).

These laws confirmed Bourbon as America's native spirit, effectively granting it a protected designation of origin that defines it clearly and means that production cannot occur abroad. On that day—as the New York World's Fair was celebrating the tricentennial of New Amsterdam coming under English control and the Beatles' "Can't Buy Me Love" saturated radio airwaves—it would have taken a lot of imagination to foresee that Bourbon would evolve into the economic engine and tourism draw that it has become.

That's because, in the 1960s, whiskey consumption was dropping rapidly in America. Baby boomers, vehemently protesting the Vietnam War and establishing their own collective identity, didn't want to drink the whiskey that their elders enjoyed. Distillers faced warehouses filled with whiskey aging for a market that didn't want it anymore. As a result, Bourbon production declined steeply. By the 1970s and '80s, the handful of Kentucky distilleries still in business resorted to diversifying their portfolios into other products, including vodka, wine, tableware, and even luggage.

Then, in the 1990s, a significant shift occurred. Consumers took an active interest in the origins of their food and drink. Kentucky Bourbon had obvious ties to its place of origin, and Bourbon drinkers wanted to see their favorite brands being made. In response to a modest but growing trickle of travelers to the state, a small group of enterprising women hatched a plan.

Peggy Noe Stevens served as director of Woodford Reserve's modest visitor center when it opened in 1996. She, Doris Calhoun at Jim Beam, and Donna Nally at Maker's Mark soon became friends. "As tourism people do, we went to travel shows, conferences, meetings, and so forth," Stevens says. "We had great camaraderie. Even though we were competitors, we enjoyed one another's company. We sipped one another's products when we were traveling together. Our jobs were to bring visitors to our distilleries, and at the time there were only seven open to the public."

Kentucky's Department of Tourism hadn't realized the industry's possible draw yet. In the 1990s, "Bourbon didn't even make the top-ten list of things to do in Kentucky," says Stevens. Getting the word out fell to the companies making the whiskey. So the trio brainstormed ways to market each of their distilleries to people who might visit only one of them. Stevens, who later founded the Bourbon Women Association, invited Calhoun and Nally to Woodford Reserve for lunch one day and discussed how they could cross-market. They wondered whether the other four Kentucky distilleries open to the public would want to participate in a mutual marketing strategy. They approached the Kentucky Distillers' Association (KDA) with their idea of a brochure promoting all the distilleries. The KDA and other distilleries liked the idea, and the Kentucky Bourbon Trail became official in 1999. The trail began with the seven distilleries offering public tours. In 2023, it featured 18 major distilleries and a Craft Tour with 19 smaller distilleries. In 2024, the KDA consolidated the craft distilleries into the main program, and more have joined its ranks since then.

A few decades ago, the industry looked like it was dying. Today, some 3 million people come to the Bluegrass State each year to travel the trail and visit non-KDA members as well, including Buffalo Trace (page 3). The Bourbon industry contributes more than $9 billion to Kentucky's economy, provides more than 23,000 jobs with a payroll of more than $2.2 billion in salaries and benefits, and generates more than $350 million in taxes for state and local governments. Kentucky accounts for about 95 percent of all Bourbon produced in America. With more than 12 million barrels of whiskey aging in rickhouses across the state, that boom shows no signs of slowing. Existing distilleries are expanding, and new distilleries are

forming. All are creating experiences for visitors that go well beyond a basic walking tour. Many have cocktail bars and restaurants, and they offer a variety of programs from "distiller for a day" to craft cocktail classes. In Louisville, Whiskey Row runs to 10 city blocks of Bourbon-related attractions, and Lexington has its Distillery District.

This book celebrates the rich histories and bright futures of these companies and their enchanting products, both stalwarts and newcomers. In it, you'll find tasting notes for worthy bottles and recommendations for Bourbon-centric restaurants and bars. Always check websites or call before visiting—especially because these businesses are developing new attractions and experiences all the time. In the 1990s, Bill Samuels Jr. of Maker's Mark predicted: "We're a small Napa Valley waiting to happen."

The wait is over.

How to Taste Bourbon

When asked how best to taste Bourbon, Beam's renowned master distiller Booker Noe gave a succinct answer: "Any damn way you like." Adding cola, ginger ale, or anything else to his product didn't faze him. He just wanted people to enjoy it. For maximum appreciation, however, keep these tips in mind.

GLASSWARE

Many Bourbon authorities favor the Glencairn glass, developed in Scotland for evaluating Scotch whisky. A small brandy snifter or tulip-shaped wineglass works well, and a regular rocks glass gets the job done, too.

COLOR

All of a Bourbon's color comes from its time in the barrel, so generally but not always, the younger the Bourbon, the lighter its color. Warehouse location can make a difference, as can secondary finishing. On the higher floors of a rickhouse, evaporation takes place more quickly, concentrating the whiskey. Finishing in a barrel that once contained a dark wine or spirit may add color, too. Higher-proof Bourbons also tend to look darker. Color can range from light straw to deep bronze.

AROMAS AND FLAVORS

In whiskey, fruity and floral aromas and flavors mostly result from fermentation. Different strains of yeast yield different esters as by-products. These aromatic compounds make apples smell like apples, bananas like bananas, and so on. For this reason, distilleries assiduously protect their proprietary yeast strains.

Caramel and vanilla—the predominant, definitive aromas and flavors in Bourbon—both come from time in the barrel. When toasting, charring, or both heat the oak, a compound called vanillin results. The heat also yields various furfurals, the origin of the caramel notes. Other barrel aromas can include a medley of baking spices, chocolate, coffee, a variety of nuts, and even some savory and smoky notes.

Tannins in the wood can impart astringency. Some tannin gives good structure. Too much can make a Bourbon taste overly woody.

TASTING BOURBON IN SIX EASY STEPS

1. Look

Hold the glass against something white, such as a napkin, tablecloth, or sheet of paper. Whether light or dark, the Bourbon should appear clear, not cloudy.

2. Swirl

This step doesn't have the same importance as it does for wine, but the thickness of legs that form on the sides of the glass indicate the Bourbon's relative viscosity, whether it will drink thin or rich. Swirling works better with the addition of a little room temperature, distilled water, especially for high-proof Bourbons. The water releases and amplifies the fruity and floral flavors.

3. Smell

Don't put your nose into the glass! That works for wine, which usually runs between 12 and 14 percent alcohol by volume. Bourbon starts at 40 percent and can exceed 65 percent! Hold the top of the glass under your nose, take a series of short sniffs, turn your head, and blow the alcohol away. Nose it a second time for lovely aromas of caramel, fruit, and spice.

4. Sip

Take a small sip and let the Bourbon travel across your mouth. Once again, turn your head and blow the alcohol away. A second small sip will reveal a much fuller array of flavors.

5. Swallow

This step reveals the characteristics of the finish. In a short finish, the flavors will fade quickly; in a long one, they'll linger. After you swallow, what flavors persist longer than others?

6. Savor

A good Bourbon maintains balance among the caramel and/or vanilla, fruit, and spices. A great Bourbon has that balance, additional complexity of flavors, a rich mouthfeel, and a long finish. To higher-proof Bourbons, adding a few drops or a squirt of water unlocks more flavors. A large ice cube achieves the same end over time. Small ice cubes will dilute Bourbon too quickly, however, and whiskey rocks or stones prove completely useless because they chill the liquid but don't otherwise enhance the flavor. Save those for your Sauvignon Blanc.

> Only you can determine how best to enjoy your Bourbon, which may depend on the expression you're sipping. In other words, just as Booker Noe said: ***"Any damn way you like."***

Price Guide

BARGAIN	$25 or less
VALUE	$25–$49.99
SPECIAL OCCASION	$50–$99.99
SPLURGE	$100 or more

Distilleries

Buffalo Trace Distillery

Founded circa 1787

BuffaloTraceDistillery.com
113 Great Buffalo Trace
Frankfort, KY 40601

Many thousands of years ago, bison herds crisscrossed the landscape, trampling paths, or traces, as they sought grazing sites and salt licks near rivers. Later, the Cherokee, Delaware, Wyandot, and other peoples established hunting camps in the area, and then European colonists arrived. An aerial view of Frankfort, Kentucky's capital, today shows a convergence of highways built over the original bison traces, native paths, and colonial roads. At a low point on the banks of the Kentucky River, one of those traces became a crossing, now the Buffalo Trace Distillery.

In 1775, brothers Willis and Hancock Lee established the Leestown settlement around the site. A year later, Willis died, but the river supplied water, which Hancock Lee used to make whiskey sometime in the late 1780s, making Buffalo Trace the state's oldest site with a history of continuous distilling.

Whiskey making continued here, steadily expanding, until 1870, when Colonel Edmund Haynes Taylor Jr. bought the property and overhauled it. He installed expensive, all-copper distilling equipment, which removes unpalatable sulfur flavors from the whiskey. Taylor renamed the distillery O.F.C., those initials still visible at the top of Warehouse C, dating from 1885. Conflicting accounts hold that the letters stand for Old Fashioned Copper or Old Fired Copper. He also introduced steam-heated warehouses, an innovation still used at Buffalo Trace and only two other Kentucky distillers, Brown-Forman and Michter's.

Taylor had a banking background but ran into financial trouble, which forced him, in 1878, to sell to George T. Stagg, one of his investors, who renamed the distillery after himself. In 1897, Stagg hired Albert Blanton, a teenage office boy. Blanton rose through the ranks to become the distillery's manager and then president of the company. He was holding the reins when, during Prohibition, the distillery became one of six in the state and 10 in the country allowed to operate and sell medicinal whiskey. The Stagg Distillery sold about 1 million bottles, each one pint as allowed by prescription.

▲ Colonel E. H. Taylor Jr.

Eventually the distillery took on Blanton's name, then Ancient Age, the flagship Bourbon made there for several decades. Elmer T. Lee, one of the facility's most revered figures, became distillery manager and eventually master distiller. In 1984, Lee innovated the release of single-barrel Bourbon, which he named Blanton's. Following the success of single-malt whisky in Scotland, that strategy, among many, aimed to reposition Bourbon as a premium spirit. With its orb-shaped bottle and stopper depicting a racehorse and jockey, Blanton's has become a much-sought brand. Lee retired in 1985 and Gary Gayheart became master distiller. Harlen Wheatley succeeded Gayheart in 2005.

In 1992, the Sazerac Company—founded in New Orleans in the mid-1800s and still privately owned— bought Ancient Age. After renovations, it reopened in 1999 as the Buffalo Trace Distillery, which today produces a large portfolio of brands. Supply for many of them routinely outstrips demand, often leading to strict allocation. In the early 2020s, Buffalo Trace doubled its distilling capacity. Each morning a select few, hard-to-find bottles—Blanton's, E. H. Taylor Bottled-in-Bond, W. L. Weller Special Reserve— appear on the shop shelves. Don't expect the limited Pappy Van Winkle expressions or the Antique Collection among them, however.

Wheatley likes to experiment. Warehouse X, a high-tech facility, allows him to track *millions* of data points—temperature, humidity, pressure, and more—as the whiskey there ages.

The distillery offers several tours, all of which include tastings. The father and grandfather of Freddie Johnson, a Kentucky Bourbon Hall of Fame tour guide, both worked at the distillery, and Johnson takes pride in the accommodations that the tours afford to visitors. "If your pets are people-friendly, they can go everywhere except into the bottling house or any place with open containers. There's a ninja playground for

the kids if they don't want to go on a tour with their parents, and we have picnic tables for them." Every year, Buffalo Trace holds an Easter egg hunt for children, and in December, Christmas lights adorn the grounds, which host a visit from Santa Claus. That family friendliness even extends to tastings. Buffalo Trace has a line of soft drinks named Freddie's that includes root beer, ginger ale, and nonalcoholic ginger beer. After the tours, anyone under age 21 gets a root beer. For legal drinkers, guides mix it with Buffalo Trace's Bourbon Cream Liqueur, which Johnson calls "the best root beer float you've ever had."

Every year, Buffalo Trace releases a trio of kosher whiskeys after Passover. The Chicago Rabbinical Council certifies the wheated Bourbon, high-rye Bourbon, and rye whiskey as kosher.

Johnson also points to the variety of tours warranting repeat visits. "We're sitting on 440 acres of land. There's enough here that, if you just want to do the history part, take the Old Taylor Tour. If you want to do the nits and grits, that's the Hard Hat Tour. They're an hour in length, with a 15-minute tasting, which gives you a chance to focus on one aspect without getting bogged down." The Trace Tour focuses on the basic functioning of the distillery, the Arboretum and Botanical Tour on the grounds, and the National Historic Landmark Tour on the full history of the company and location.

The grounds contain plenty of attractions. A little café in the former distillery firehouse serves barbecue sandwiches from late spring into early fall with outdoor seating. An on-site facility repairs barrels that become damaged during transport or leaky from aging. Between the visitor center and the distillery, a trompe l'oeil mural depicts the interior of a warehouse that seems to shift perspective as you walk past. Opposite the mural stands a two-story log house that Albert Blanton had moved onto the property as the employ-

ees' lunch facility. Today, it serves as an events space hosting private dinners and weddings. Perhaps the most unique feature lies at the other end the pavement from the front of the visitor center: the world's smallest whiskey warehouse. Warehouse V holds exactly one barrel of Bourbon. Every time a millionth barrel rolls off the production line, it goes here for maturation and, after aging, into commemorative bottles for sale or donated to charities for fund-raising.

Recommended Bottles

Category designations follow Buffalo Trace's suggested retail prices. Some retailers mark up these brands considerably, so don't be surprised if you see a value expression at a special occasion price—or more. Markups often gouge the annual releases of the Antique Collection.

BARGAIN
Benchmark Full Proof
Ancient Age

VALUE
Buffalo Trace
Weller Special Reserve
Sazerac Rye

SPECIAL OCCASION
Weller 12 Year
Blanton's Single Barrel
Weller Antique
Eagle Rare 10 Year
Van Winkle Special Reserve
Col. E. H. Taylor, Jr. Small Batch
Stagg, Jr.
Rock Hill Farm

SPLURGE
Pappy Van Winkle Family Reserve 15 Year Old
Pappy Van Winkle Family Reserve 20 Year Old
Antique Collection, any: Eagle Rare 17 Year Old, George T. Stagg, William Larue Weller, Thomas H. Handy Rye, and Sazerac Rye 18 Year Old

Tasting Notes

Buffalo Trace doesn't release details about mash bills, except that they use three for the Bourbons. Number 1 has more malted barley than Number 2, which has more rye than Number 1. The Weller and van Winkle Bourbons use wheat instead of rye.

BENCHMARK FULL PROOF

BT mash bill #1, no age statement, 62.5% ABV (125 proof)

On the nose, caramel, raisins, plums, and dates, plus a little baking spice and oak, carry through to the palate, where it tastes warm but not hot. It has a long, peppery finish.

BUFFALO TRACE

BT mash bill #1, no age statement, 45% ABV (90 proof)

It smells and tastes of pears and apples, with dark brown sugar, honey, vanilla, leather, and a bit of pipe tobacco. A medley of baking spices contributes to the overall balance before it dries to an oak-and-spice finish.

WELLER 12-YEAR

Wheated mash bill, 12 years old, 45% ABV (90 proof)

It has aromas and flavors of vanilla, light brown sugar, and ripe apples, with roasted pecans and cinnamon sugar. As it opens, the brown sugar grows into caramel. If left long enough, it becomes rich toffee.

BLANTON'S SINGLE BARREL

BT mash bill #2, no age statement, 46.5% ABV (93 proof)

Aromas include crème brûlée and ripe apples with a dusting of cinnamon sugar. Underneath the fruit and cinnamon, a nice note of book leather and nutmeg contributes to the spice. It drinks notably smooth and rich.

COL. E. H. TAYLOR, JR. SMALL BATCH

BT mash bill #1, at least 4 years old, 50% ABV (100 proof)

Caramel corn, apples, and honey compose the base with layers of sweet tobacco, hazelnuts, nutmeg, and a touch of oak. Some cherries emerge with a few drops of water or an ice cube. Complex and very smooth.

PAPPY VAN WINKLE 15-YEAR-OLD

Wheated mash bill, 15 years old, 53.5% ABV (107 proof)

It smells of caramel, pears, green apple, dark honey, and warm caramel sauce, becoming especially fruity with marzipan, cinnamon, and dark cherries on the palate. Notes of saddle leather and oak carry through the finish, which has a nice spike of pepper.

GEORGE T. STAGG

BT mash bill #1, unchill filtered, at least 15 years old, proof varies

It begins with toffee and chocolate, like a liquid Heath bar. Then dark fruit—black currants, blackberries, raisins—join notes of tobacco and some espresso bean. With a little water, the notes emerge in succession, like Russian nesting dolls. Exceptionally complex and rich.

BOURBON POMPEII

Nick Laracuente has a job that probably exists only in Kentucky: Bourbon archaeologist. Buffalo Trace called him before excavating under the oldest building on the distillery site, the Commodore Richard Taylor House, built in 1792. Laracuente's digging unearthed Native American artifacts, including sharpened stone points perhaps used to hunt the bison that crossed the river here.

But Laracuente's work didn't end there. A few yards away stood a large storage building. The distillery started to convert it to an event space, but when workers jack-hammered the concrete floor, they discovered ruins underneath it that included copper-lined fermentation vats from Colonel Taylor's O.F.C. Distillery.

The company shelved plans for the event space there and proceeded with a full excavation of the location. The unearthed ruins, nicknamed "Bourbon Pompeii," form the heart of the Old Taylor Tour. To view the vestiges of the old distillery, you traverse catwalks, and plaques describing Taylor's time there line the pathway. Buffalo Trace even put one of the excavated fermentation vats back in use. Once again, it ferments Taylor's 150-year-old Bourbon recipe.

Old Forester Distilling Company

Founded in 1870

OldForester.com
117–119 West Main Street
Louisville, KY 40202

In 1870, George Garvin Brown, a 23-year-old pharmaceutical salesman in Louisville, was hearing complaints from his physician customers of inconsistent quality in the Bourbon he was selling them. In those days, whiskey qualified as medicine, so pharmaceutical salesmen also sold Bourbon. Doctors and dentists commonly purchased a barrel and dispensed the liquid to patients as needed. Brown and others bought Bourbon from dealers called rectifiers, but the contents could vary considerably. Rectifiers often sourced whiskey from multiple distilleries, blended it, and added coloring and flavoring agents, such as tea and prune juice. They also might add neutral grain spirits or even kerosene to stretch the whiskey without diluting the alcohol.

Brown wanted to keep his clients satisfied, so he started his own rectifying company with John Thompson Street Brown, his half brother, and sourced Bourbon from the Atherton and Mellwood Distilleries in Louisville and Mattingly Distillery in Marion County. He batched to exacting standards and sold his Bourbon exclusively in sealed glass bottles. Manufacturers weren't mass-producing bottles yet, so those vessels increased the cost of production. Brown gambled that his customers would pay more for a product that they could trust. As a quality guarantee, he signed each label and astutely named his Bourbon Old Forrester, with prominent Louisville physician William Forrester lending his name to the product in exchange for a share of the profits. If the whiskey had a doctor's name on it, it had to be excellent medicine, right?

One *r* eventually dropped from the name, but the brand endured. Indeed, it remains the only Bourbon sold under the same name by the same company before Prohibition, through Prohibition, to present day. Brown's bet that people would pay more for reliable whiskey paid in spades. His rectifying company evolved into Brown-Forman, a spirits powerhouse that also makes Woodford Reserve (page 75) and Jack Daniels Tennessee Whiskey.

In 1882, the company's offices moved into adjacent buildings at 117 and 119 West Main Street, part of Lou-

isville's Whiskey Row (page 199). Brown continued buying whiskey from distilleries until 1901 when he bought the Mattingly Distillery and Brown-Forman started distilling its own Bourbon. Brown died in 1917, and his son Owsley took over. Two years later, Prohibition forced the Main Street offices to close,

> Many Louisvillians consider Old Forester their hometown Bourbon, shortening the name to "Old Fo."

but Owsley Brown secured one of the 10 federal permits for distilleries to make, store, and sell whiskey to drugstores for medicinal purposes.

In 1933, Congress repealed Prohibition, and the company resumed growing, starting with going public that year. Brown-Forman stock trades on the New York Stock Exchange, but Brown family members remain majority stockholders. In 1940, the Old Kentucky Distillery in Shively, just southwest of Louisville, joined the fold. After the Japanese attack on Pearl Harbor, it became the first distillery to convert all production to industrial alcohol for the war effort. A newer facility replaced that distillery in the 1950s,

and it expanded in the following decade, including landscaping by Olmsted Associates of New York, who famously had designed Central Park and Louisville's parks system. Private barrel selections once took place in the Shively distillery, which never offered public tours.

Starting in 1959 and for more than 40 years, the drinking public could enjoy only Old Forester Classic, with a mash bill of 72 percent corn, 18 percent rye, 10 percent malted barley; barrel-aged for between four and six years; and bottled at 43 percent ABV (86 proof). In 2002, the company issued its first Birthday Bourbon, always available on or near Sep-

tember 2, George Garvin Brown's birthday. Very limited, it has the same mash bill as the Classic, but aging time, usually in double digits, varies from year to year. In 2014, Brown-Forman purchased the buildings on West Main Street that had housed George Garvin Brown's offices a century earlier, and Old Forester introduced the Whiskey Row Series, with each expression commemorating a significant date in the distillery's history. The next year, Campbell Brown, a great-great-grandson of the company's founder, became president and managing director.

The 70,000-square-foot Old Forester Distillery opened in 2018 and offers a historic tour of the company and production process from fermentation to storage. At a mini on-site cooperage, you can watch coopers raising and charring barrels, which no other distillery tour in the state features, an appropriate extra because Brown-Forman owned its own cooperage in Louisville until 2025. Other distilleries buy their barrels from large cooperages, such as Independent Stave Company. The Main Street building also houses an urban rickhouse containing ricks made of steel instead of wood. Private barrel selections now happen here, on a platform suspended in the middle of the rickhouse. At the end of the standard tour, tastings take place in the room that once served as George Garvin Brown's office. You don't need to take a tour, though, to visit the distillery shop or enjoy a drink in George's Bar, which offers custom cocktails that make the most of Old Forester.

Along the backs of the warehouses, the 1960s Olmsted design planted white oaks in stately rows. The White Oak Initiative, a project overseen by the University of Kentucky's Department of Forestry and Natural Resources, studies the preservation of that tree species, which, in barrel form, proves crucial to the Bourbon industry. As part of that program, the company started the Old Forester Tree Nursery in 2021 to study tree growth in an urban habitat.

Recommended Bottles

BARGAIN
Old Forester Classic
Old Forester Signature

VALUE
Old Forester Whiskey Row 1920

SPECIAL OCCASION
Old Forester Whiskey Row 1910

SPLURGE
Old Forester Whiskey Row 1924
Old Forester Birthday Bourbon

Tasting Notes

With the exception of Whiskey Row 1924, all Old Forester expressions use the same mash bill—72 percent corn, 18 percent rye, 10 percent malted barley—and the same proprietary yeast strain. All age in heat-cycled warehouses. Most Kentucky distilleries don't control temperatures in their rickhouses. Instead, they rely on seasonal fluctuations to expand and contract the barrels. In addition to the Whiskey Row Series, other limited releases include President's Choice, selected by Campbell Brown and Melissa Rift, and the 117 Series sold in 375-milliliter bottles and available only at the shop on Main Street.

OLD FORESTER CLASSIC

43% ABV (86 proof)

Complex aromas include lots of caramel, baking spices, and fruit, especially banana—a signature of the Old Forester yeast strain—and some orange. Caramel, fruit, and notes of cinnamon sugar carry to the palate. A balanced stand-alone sip, it also makes outstanding cocktails.

OLD FORESTER
WHISKEY ROW 1870

45% ABV (90 proof)

Expect plenty of toffee, berries, and apples, and an almost chewy mouthfeel. Imagine drinking apple pie drizzled generously with caramel. The year commemorates the founding of the brand.

OLD FORESTER
WHISKEY ROW 1897

50% ABV (100 proof)

It evokes banana, cinnamon, vanilla, caramel, and baking spices—in other words, bananas Foster with Bourbon instead of rum. This bottled-in-bond expression honors the year that Congress passed the Bottled-in-Bond Act.

OLD FORESTER
WHISKEY ROW 1910

46.5% ABV (93 proof)

In 1910, a fire on the bottling line forced Bourbon already dumped for bottling back into barrels. This expression aged an extra 18 months in second barrels charred so deeply that the flame extinguishes just before the wood turns to ash. As a result, it features savory flavors of light smoke, chocolate, and even a hint of bacon.

OLD FORESTER
WHISKEY ROW 1920

57.5% ABV (115 proof)

Prohibition took effect in 1920, but Old Forester remained one of 10 distilleries in the country legally allowed to make and sell whiskey. It has aromas and flavors of caramel, a hint of tobacco, ripe apple, berries, and baking spices. Add a little water to amplify the fruit, spice, and bold nuttiness.

OLD FORESTER
WHISKEY ROW 1924

79% corn, 11% rye, 10% malted barley, 50% ABV (100 proof)

Across Kentucky, Prohibition shuttered more than 200 distilleries, most with warehouses full of whiskey that, unguarded, had a way of disappearing. In 1924, the federal government ordered the consolidation of those barrels into the six Kentucky distilleries operating with medicinal permits. As a result, Old Forester was selling whiskey that it hadn't made but that bore its label, hence the different mash bill. It imparts complex notes of vanilla wafer and graham cracker joined by milk chocolate, marzipan, cinnamon, sweet cherries, and orange peel.

MASTER TASTER MELISSA RIFT

Born in Louisville, Melissa Rift moved with her family to Dallas at age 11. She returned to earn her master's degree in social work. In graduate school, she helped cover her living expenses by giving weekend tours at the Stitzel-Weller Distillery (page 53). London-based spirits giant Diageo owned the distillery founded by Julian "Pappy" Van Winkle and, when Rift worked there, the Bulleit brand. When Diageo built the new Bulleit Distillery east of Louisville, she moved there and headed developing visitor experiences, including barrel selections, tastings, and tours. After a stint with Beam Suntory, she became master taster at Old Forester in 2022.

In that capacity, she participates in two sides of the industry. "There's the production side and the marketing side," she says. "But Brown-Forman does a good job of bridging that." She spends almost half of her time traveling, as the face of the brand, to help bartenders and other hospitality staff understand the various expressions. She soon found herself at Tales of the Cocktail in New Orleans, Portland Cocktail Week, San Diego Bartenders' Weekend, and other substantial markets, including New York and Las Vegas.

For the other portion of her job, she helps develop new expressions, fine-tunes existing ones, and guides tastings for private barrel selections. People frequently ask about her path to this high-profile position as a woman in an industry perceived widely as being male dominated. "I always start by saying that there's been a first and second guard of women who kicked the door down and paved the way. I have massive respect for Peggy Noe Stevens [the industry's first woman master taster], Marianne Eaves [former assistant master distiller at Brown-Forman], and Jackie"

Zykan, Rift's immediate predecessor as master taster. "They did the legwork to create these spaces and opportunities, and I've been fortunate enough to come behind and reinforce them."

Rift also defies another Bourbon industry stereotype. She's openly a lesbian—and she's not alone. "I recently joined the board of Queer Kentucky, a nonprofit education and cultural impact organization. Someone there asked me if there were a lot of queer people working in Bourbon, and I said, 'Oh yeah.' The service industry has such a vibrant queer community that we have a lot of opportunity as a supplier to reach out and collaborate a bit more with those spaces, which I hope to do. It's been great to have allies and other queer folks. I walked in the Pride Parade with Brown-Forman, the first time I got to walk with my employer, which was very special for me. Representation matters, so if you've got folks who appreciate drinking fine whiskey and they see someone from their community in a position of spokesmanship, they'd be more inclined to support that brand and feel safe with them."

Green River Distilling Company

Founded in 1885

GreenRiverDistilling.com
10 Distillery Road
Owensboro, KY 42301

In 1859, T. J. Monarch and C. L. Hagen built the first distillery associated with Green River. John McCulloch, a government agent working as a tax gauger, entered the business at age 25 when, in 1885, he bought the distillery. McCulloch moved the distillery to its current site in 1900, enjoying considerable success with the Green River brand. The logo featured a horseshoe, presumably for luck—but with mixed results.

Production grew steadily for 18 years, gaining national recognition and becoming the official whiskey for the US Public Health & Marine Hospital Service. It also had maybe the best advertising slogan for a Bourbon ever: "The Whiskey without a Headache." Promises, promises. During this period, company brands included Mountain Dew and Kentucky Moonshine.

In August 1918, the distillery and its warehouses containing 43,000 barrels of Bourbon conveniently burned down with Prohibition scheduled to take effect in just five months. McCulloch hadn't been able to obtain one of the few, coveted federal licenses to sell medical whiskey, but he had insured his distillery fully. He died in 1927, at age 67, with Prohibition still the law of the land. The company rebuilt in 1937, but new laws forbade advertising from attributing health benefits to alcohol, forcing a change of slogan: "The Whiskey without Regrets." Pretty good and still used for Green River Bourbons and rye today.

After being rebuilt, the distillery changed ownership and names several times, becoming the Medley Distillery, Glenmore Distillery, and O. Z. Tyler Distillery, then finally reverting to Green River in 2020. Bardstown Bourbon Company bought it two years

later. Today, in the distillation room, you'll see the handsome copper pot doubler installed by distiller Charles Medley, but not a striking copper-and-blue column still that he also used and had to replace after a 1999 tornado damaged it. (Someone wasn't polishing that horseshoe.) Green River's core whiskeys consist of a high-rye Bourbon, a wheated Bourbon, and a rye.

Tasting Notes

GREEN RIVER KENTUCKY STRAIGHT BOURBON

70% corn, 21% rye, 9% malted barley, no age statement, 45% ABV (90 proof)

It offers brown sugar, candied orange peel, some cinnamon, and cardamom. As it sits, peaches emerge before yielding to baking spice and light oak on the finish.

GREEN RIVER KENTUCKY STRAIGHT WHEATED BOURBON

70% corn, 21% soft red winter wheat, 9% malted barley, no age statement, 45% ABV (90 proof)

It smells and tastes of rich caramel with some apricot, peaches, cinnamon, and hazelnuts. A smooth sip neat or with an ice cube.

O. H. INGRAM RIVER AGED BOURBON WHISKEY

Wheated (proportions not released), no age statement, 52.5% ABV (105 proof)

It suggests caramel and vanilla wafers with canned peach syrup, cinnamon, and even banana. A lovely dessert Bourbon with an ice cube that makes the fruit the star.

BUZZARD'S ROOST CHAR #1 BOURBON

60% corn, 36% rye, 4% malted barley, 4 years old, 52.5% ABV (105 proof)

On the nose and palate, you'll find warm toffee with cardamom, cinnamon, dark cherries, and figs. Notes of milk chocolate and vanilla wafer arise, too, as do apple and sweet malt. It has a long, nutty finish.

BUZZARD'S ROOST TOASTED AMERICAN OAK STRAIGHT BOURBON

Blend of two mash bills: 75% corn, 21% rye, 4% malted barley and 60% corn, 36% rye, 4% malted barley, 4 and 5 years old, 52.5% ABV (105 proof)

Aromas include crème brûlée with notes of honey, candied orange peel, a whiff of coconut, and some grated nutmeg. On the palate, a bit of butterscotch shows up along with a dash of white pepper and some light oak.

CONTRACT DISTILLING

Brand ambassador Caryn Wells notes that, like parent company Bardstown Bourbon, Green River produces a lot of whiskey for other companies that don't have their own facilities. "About 75 percent of what we do is contract distilling," she says. "The two biggest are O. H. Ingram and Buzzard's Roost. The other 25 percent is Green River."

After Green River distills O. H. Ingram's whiskey, the barrels ship to the client's floating warehouse on the Mississippi River, a barge as rickhouse moored on the Kentucky shore at Columbus. The gentle rocking of the barge moves the whiskey into and out of the walls of the barrels during aging. For more information, visit IngramWhiskey.com.

From Green River's column still, some of the first distillation goes to Louisville for second distillation in the Buzzard's Roost doubler. The client brand uses 17 proprietary barrels toasted and charred in various ways to achieve desired flavor extractions. In its location on Louisville's Whiskey Row, Buzzard's Roost also has a tasting room and cocktail bar (page 201). For more information, visit BuzzardsRoostWhiskey.com.

Four Roses Distillery

Founded in 1888

FourRosesBourbon.com
1224 Bonds Mill Road
Lawrenceburg, KY 40342

After the Civil War, Paul Jones and son Paul Jr. moved from Virginia to Atlanta and built a successful business as whiskey dealers. But by 1883, Georgia was experiencing a strong temperance movement, so the Joneses decamped to Tennessee. A few years later, noting the growing concentration of whiskey dealers on Louisville's West Main Street—now Whiskey Row (page 199)—they moved to Kentucky. By 1888, they had acquired the stocks of Four Roses Bourbon from distiller R. M. Rose.

> Paul Jones Sr.'s son Colonel Warner P. Jones commanded Confederate troops at the Battle of Perryville, the most significant Civil War battle in Kentucky and now a historic site about 30 miles southwest of the distillery. Kentucky remained in the Union, whose forces won the battle.

One version of the origin story of the brand's name holds that Rose was honoring his four daughters. Another posits that a cousin of the Joneses was courting a Georgia woman who had refused several of his marriage proposals. Making one last attempt, he invited her to a ball and asked that she arrive wearing a corsage of four roses if her answer was yes, which, according to distillery lore, she did. No one knows the precise origins of the name.

When Prohibition went into effect, Paul Jones Jr. obtained one of the 10 licenses the federal government granted nationwide to sell medicinal whiskey. Jones moved his holdings from Louisville to Frankfort and opened Frankfort Distilleries, which bottled and sold Paul Jones, Antique, and Four Roses. After Repeal, the Jones family ran the distillery for another decade before selling it to Canadian spirits company Seagram.

In 1920, the year that Prohibition began, a racehorse named after Paul Jones Bourbon won the Kentucky Derby. That year, Man o' War won the Preakness and the Belmont, but his owners hadn't entered him in the Derby.

At the same time, Seagram was buying four other distilleries, including Old Prentice in Lawrenceburg, which John Thompson Street Brown of Old Forester had built in 1910. The Spanish Mission–style complex of buildings cuts a strikingly odd figure in the Kentucky countryside, and no one knows why Brown chose that style of architecture. Seagram moved the Four Roses brand to the Old Prentice Distillery, but the Canadian conglomerate brought more than just a change of location to Four Roses, which had become a well-regarded, strong-selling brand. Old Prentice turned it into a cheap blended whiskey, mixing it with grain neutral spirits, which meant that was no longer classified legally as Bourbon. The distillery continued making premium Bourbon for export to Japan and Europe, however.

In the late 1990s, Seagram suffered financial collapse and sold off the four distilleries that it had acquired at the same time as Four Roses, which is

how the Lawrenceburg facility came to have today's five yeast strains and two mash bills. Jim Rutledge, a longtime Seagram employee, became master distiller in 1994 and singlehandedly kept the Four Roses brand alive. Seagram sold the Old Prentice Distillery, which Japan's Kirin Company bought in 2002, allowing Four Roses to begin its comeback.

Rutledge disliked that Americans couldn't buy Four Roses, so he convinced the new owners to drop the bottom-shelf blended whiskey and relaunch the brand in America as a proper Bourbon. He introduced the 80-proof expression, which many fans still call "Yellow Label" even though the color changed to beige in 2018. He also launched Four Roses Single Barrel at 50 percent ABV (100 proof), using only one of the distillery's ten recipes, and the Small Batch, which uses four recipes.

In 2015, Brent Elliott succeeded Rutledge as master distiller. Several years later, Elliott added Four Roses Small Batch Select, a mingling of six recipes, to the mix. "It was the first permanent new expression since we released Small Batch in 2006," Elliot says. He also confesses to doing some soul-searching during the Bourbon's development. "We wanted something that would appeal to the more modern Bourbon consumer who's looking for something higher proof and something non-chill filtered. So we ended up with 104 proof. We wanted to expand on our uniqueness, which is our ability to use the ten recipes in different ways to create truly different expressions. That was what I was working with, and those were the boundaries. I was tasked with creating a flavor profile much different from any of the other expressions."

As master distiller, Elliott also selects barrels for limited, annual, small-batch releases, and he occasionally takes part in private barrel selections, a sometimes complicated process because selectors may face ten barrels in the tasting room, each containing a different cask strength recipe.

With the growing popularity of Bourbon tourism, the distillery's visitor center has enlarged and undergone remodeling several times. Among other items, the gift shop offers a sampler pack of 50-milliliter bottles of all 10 recipes. The facility also contains a cocktail bar, lounge, and spaces for tastings and cocktail classes. Four Roses also leans into its name. The

grounds feature plenty of rosebushes, and scattered on counters and tabletops throughout the visitor center and offices, you'll find small vases containing quartets of freshly cut roses. (The center's florist must have an excellent budget.) The rickhouses across the road from Four Roses belong to Wild Turkey (page 27). Four Roses ages its Bourbon in warehouses on a separate campus.

Recommended Bottles

BARGAIN
Four Roses

VALUE
Four Roses Single Barrel
Four Roses Small Batch

SPECIAL OCCASION
Four Roses Small Batch Select

SPLURGE
Limited annual releases, any
Barrel-strength private selections of individual
 recipes, any

Tasting Notes

Four Roses, the last distillery belonging to Seagram and now owned by Kirin, uses two mash bills and five yeast strains, which, combined, can make 10 different recipes used singly or in various proportions across all expressions. Each recipe receives a four-letter code. "O," the first letter, stands for Old Prentice Distillery. The second letter indicates the mash bill: "E," with 75 percent corn, 20 percent rye, 5 percent malted barley; or "B," with 60 percent corn, 35 percent rye, 5 percent malted barley. Mash bill "B" has one of the highest rye contents of any Bourbon. The third letter, "S," abbreviates "straight" to indicate straight Bourbon: aged at least two years with no coloring, flavoring, or other spirits added. The fourth letter signifies the yeast strain: "F" for herbal notes, "K" for light spices, "O" for rich fruit, "Q" for floral essence, and "V" for delicate fruit. Spelled out, the 10 possibilities consist of the following:

Code	Distillery	Mash Bill	Category	Yeast Strain
OBSF	Old Prentice	60% corn, 35% rye	straight	herbal
OBSK	Old Prentice	60% corn, 35% rye	straight	light spices
OBSO	Old Prentice	60% corn, 35% rye	straight	rich fruit
OBSQ	Old Prentice	60% corn, 35% rye	straight	floral
OBSV	Old Prentice	60% corn, 35% rye	straight	delicate fruit
OESF	Old Prentice	75% corn, 20% rye	straight	herbal
OESK	Old Prentice	75% corn, 20% rye	straight	light spices
OESO	Old Prentice	75% corn, 20% rye	straight	rich fruit
OESQ	Old Prentice	75% corn, 20% rye	straight	floral
OESV	Old Prentice	75% corn, 20% rye	straight	delicate fruit

FOUR ROSES

All 10 recipes possible, at least 5 years old, 40% ABV (80 proof)

The impressively flavorful flagship expression goes into the bottle at the minimum ABV required by law. Expect very floral aromas and flavors with vanilla and brown sugar providing the base, over which a medley of pears, apples, and berries lightly dances. It makes an excellent Old-Fashioned.

FOUR ROSES SINGLE BARREL

OBSV, 7 to 9 years old, 50% ABV (100 proof)

Complex and with a rich mouthfeel, it evokes sweet berries, apples, and pears with a hint of milk chocolate and rich crème brûlée. The long finish ends with a flourish of cinnamon spice. It drinks smooth enough to enjoy neat.

FOUR ROSES SMALL BATCH

OBSO, OBSK, OESO, OESK; 6 to 7 years old, 45% ABV (90 proof)

Blackberries and black currants with a fragrant mix of baking spices and vanilla pudding make this expression a fine after-dinner sip, like dessert in a glass. A pinch of pepper punctuates the long finish.

FOUR ROSES SMALL BATCH SELECT

OBSV, OESV, OBSK, OESK, OBSF, OESF; 6 to 7 years old, 52% ABV (104 proof)

Honeysuckle and roses on the nose join dark brown sugar, allspice, vanilla, butterscotch, nuts, and cherries on the palate. A drop or two of water or one ice cube spurs a ripening of the fruit and blossoming of the flowers.

Wild Turkey Distilling Company

Founded in 1891

WildTurkeyBourbon.com
1417 Versailles Road
Lawrenceburg, KY 40342

In the 1830s, James Ripy and his brother John emigrated from County Tyrone in Ireland. On the Kentucky River, between Lawrenceburg and Versailles, they opened a general store, establishing the town of Streamville. In 1868, James and two business partners bought a distillery there, and some 15 years later, the names of both the distillery and the town changed to Tyrone. Ripy eventually bought at least three more distilleries in the area. His son Thomas B. Ripy ran one of them, Cliff Springs. In 1891, James acquired a distillery, which he tore down and replaced with a new brick facility that became the progenitor of Wild Turkey.

In 1888, Thomas B. Ripy built a 30-room, Queen Anne–style mansion on Main Street in Lawrenceburg. At 11,000 square feet, it features 14-foot ceilings, stained-glass windows, walnut and mahogany woodwork, and cast-iron fireplace mantels decorated with gold leaf. Open to the public, the T. B. Ripy Home hosts a variety of Bourbon events. For more information, visit TBRipyHome.com.

Since then, a succession of distilleries has occupied the bluff overlooking the Kentucky River where Wild Turkey stands today, and the Ripy family owned or operated most of them. The family eventually became the area's largest employer. By 1906, the facility in question was operating as the Ripy Bros. Distillery, but its prosperity proved short-lived. Prohibition shuttered Ripy Bros. in 1920, and the distillery building was torn down, though not the warehouses.

Rebuilt and reopened after Prohibition, the distillery manufactured whiskey for clients to distribute and resell. One of the largest of those clients was Austin Nichols & Co., a New York City wholesale grocer. Some accounts relate that in 1940 Thomas McCarthy, an Austin Nichols executive, liked to hunt in Kentucky. He filled easy-to-carry flasks from the Ripy warehouses and supplied his turkey-hunting companions with barrel-proof Bourbon. They liked it and reportedly asked when he could get "more of that wild turkey Bourbon." By 1942, Austin Nichols was distributing Wild Turkey Bourbon nationally.

Name changes continued. In 1954, Jimmy Russell, a 19-year-old from nearby Lawrenceburg, was hired on at the Anderson Co. Distilling Co., as it was known then, to sweep floors. Russell recently had married Joretta Freeman, a secretary at the distillery who knew of the job opening. Russell quickly moved from sweeping to excelling at a variety of tasks. In 1967, he became master distiller at J. T. S. Brown & Sons, as it had become. In 1971, Austin Nichols bought the distillery outright, which now bore the name of Wild Turkey, the flagship brand. Starting that year, Wild Turkey released ceramic decanters to bolster sales, inevitably depicting one or more turkeys. The gimmick never succeeded—with the line discontinued in 1989—but the decanters have become collector's items, especially valuable if sealed and still containing whiskey.

Russell always relied on one Bourbon mash bill: 75 percent corn, 13 percent rye, 12 percent malted barley. He aged Wild Turkey 101, which made the brand's reputation, for eight years, which he long has advocated as the aging "sweet spot." Some years ago, the brand removed that age statement from the bottles, but some Bourbon that age probably forms part of each batch. In 1976, the distillery tried its hand at innovation with Wild Turkey Liqueur, a Bourbon cousin of Drambuie, the first such spirit to use Bourbon. Today, you can buy it as Wild Turkey Honey.

In 1981, Eddie Russell joined his father, following in his footsteps, performing a variety of jobs, and absorbing the details of the operation as his father continued expanding the portfolio.

Starting in 1989, with Wild Turkey Rare Breed, the company introduced new expressions of varying ages and proofs. Eddie spearheaded Russell's Reserve, released in 2001, became associate master distiller in 2008, and co-master distiller, alongside his father, in 2015.

Changes in ownership also continued. Grupo Campari acquired Wild Turkey in 2009. The Italian spir-

its conglomerate demolished the cramped, antiquated facility and built a new, state-of-the-art distillery just up the hill, which doubled distilling capacity. Campari's investment exceeded a new distillery, though. It built an enormous new visitor center to replace the little house that had served that purpose since Wild Turkey first opened for tours. Constructed to resemble a large tobacco barn, the iconic structure recently underwent extensive renovation. When the building reopened in spring 2024, it became the Jimmy Russell Wild Turkey Experience in honor of the legendary master distiller.

THREE GENERATIONS OF RUSSELLS

In October 2023, luminaries gathered for dinner at Barn8, a restaurant luxuriously remodeled from a former thoroughbred barn on the historic Hermitage Farm, east of Louisville. The occasion marked the release of Generations, a limited-edition Bourbon blended from barrels chosen by three generations of the Russell family—Jimmy, Eddie, and Bruce, Eddie's son and an associate blender at Wild Turkey—and paid tribute to patriarch, Jimmy, to celebrate his 70th year at the distillery, making him the longest serving master distiller in Bourbon history.

Current and retired master distillers, representatives from the Kentucky Distillers' Association, and prominent whiskey journalists dined on Russell family favorites, including country ham and pimento cheese biscuits, turkey hash, and soup beans with fried cornbread. Jim Beam master distiller Fred Noe, Eddie and Bruce Russell, and JoAnn Street, Eddie's niece and a Wild Turkey brand ambassador, spoke eloquently about the man of the hour. Eddie and Bruce also described the creation of the blend.

The eldest Russell chose the youngest Bourbon from barrels ranging in age from 6 to 12 years. Eddie favored a 15-year Bourbon, and his son picked the oldest barrel at 16 years. Bottled at 60 percent ABV (120 proof), the final expression tasted every bit as complex as you might expect from the esteemed palates responsible for it, with heady aromas of honeysuckle, cloves, baked apples, and rich toffee on the nose. The palate offered dense vanilla fudge with caramel sauce topped with Luxardo cherries and accented with some pepper and oak, which joined coffee with cream on the finish.

The remodeled center features a partially covered terrace and bar overlooking the tree-covered palisades of the Kentucky River. Through walls of windows, a second-floor retail shop and cocktail lounge also offer must-see vistas from the historic bluff. A portion of the copper column still from the old distillery stands as the centerpiece of that room.

Wild Turkey continues to expand. In 2023, ground broke for a second distillery scheduled to open in 2025. It will be able to produce more than 5 million gallons of whiskey, increasing Wild Turkey's distilling capacity to about 14 million gallons.

Recommended Bottles

BARGAIN
Wild Turkey 101
Wild Turkey Rye

VALUE
Wild Turkey Rare Breed
Russell's Reserve 10 Year

SPECIAL OCCASION
Wild Turkey Kentucky Spirit
Russell's Reserve Single Barrel

SPLURGE
Wild Turkey Master's Keep
Wild Turkey Generations

Tasting Notes

All Wild Turkey Bourbons have a mash bill of 75 percent corn, 13 percent rye, 12 percent malted barley.

WILD TURKEY 101

no age statement (batches include 6 to 8 years), 50.5% ABV (101 proof)
It features aromas of fine leather, caramel, and vanilla, with a whiff of tobacco leaf and a little honey and, on the palate, cherries, berries, and some citrus. The long, smooth finish ends with a drop of honey.

WILD TURKEY RARE BREED

58.4% ABV (116.8 proof) (varies by release)
It imparts dark fruit, caramel, almonds, and vanilla on the nose. The fruit lightens to apricots and peaches on the velvety palate with brown sugar, allspice, and some sweet oak. The long finish has some sweet tobacco and, with the addition of water, becomes even longer with baking spices.

RUSSELL'S RESERVE 10 YEAR

10 years old, 45% ABV (90 proof)
It offers marzipan, vanilla, and milk chocolate on the nose, along with some sweet spices and cherry that carry to the palate, where rich caramel accompanies them. The long finish ends with some nuts. Balanced and elegant.

RUSSELL'S RESERVE SINGLE BARREL

no age statement, 55% ABV (110 proof)
It smells complex and powerful: toffee, pecans, dark honey, molasses, honeycomb, and some saddle leather. Dried cherries develop on the palate, which a little water will intensify. A rich, rounded finish lingers well past all expectation.

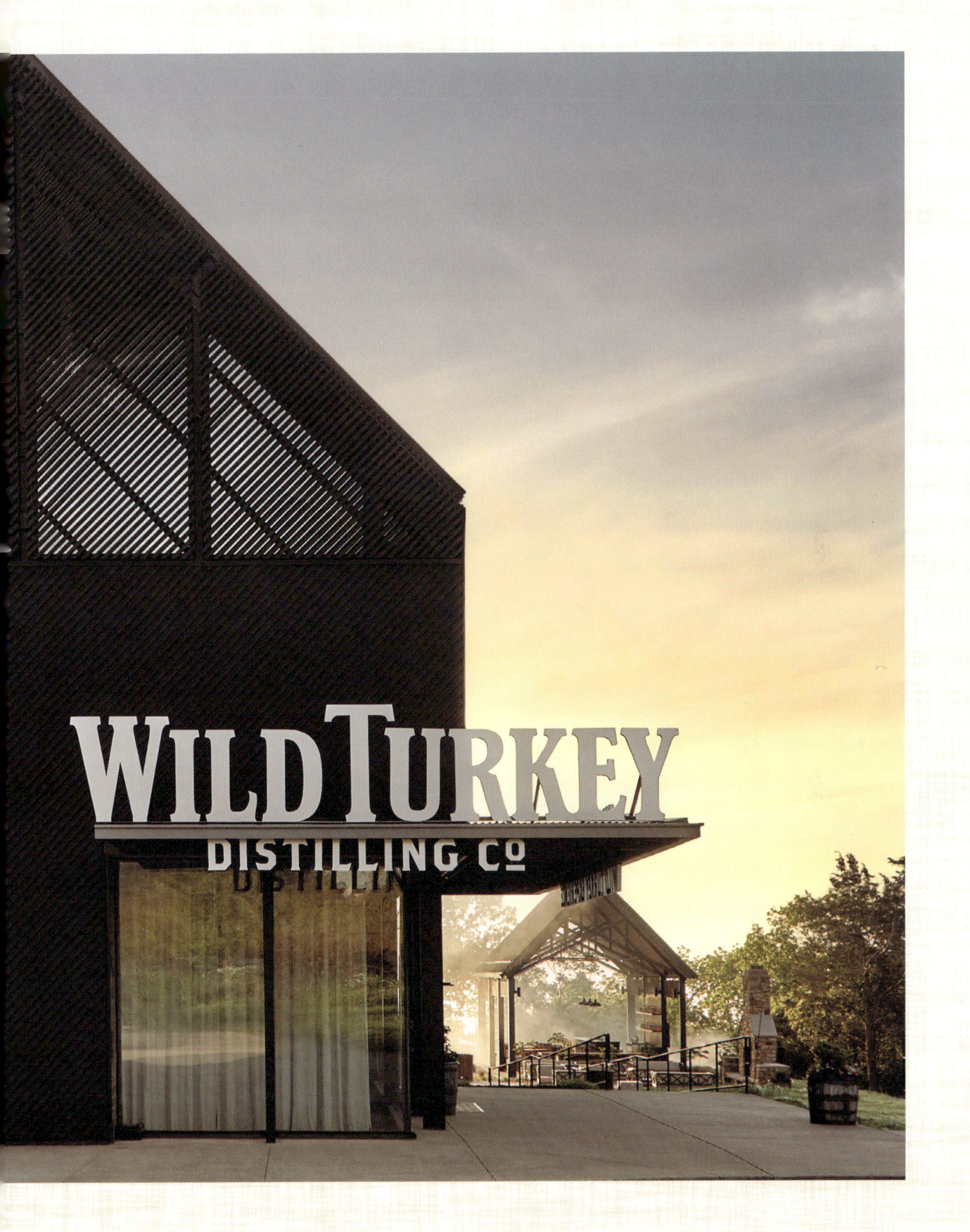

James B. Beam Distilling Company

Founded in 1934

JimBeam.com
568 Happy Hollow Road
Clermont, KY 40110

S oon after he arrived in Kentucky in 1788, Johannes Jacob Boehm became known as Jacob Beam. Some accounts identify him as a German immigrant. Others hold that he was born in Pennsylvania to German-immigrant parents. Either way, like many farmers in the 1700s and early 1800s, he also milled grain and distilled it. After Beam; his wife, Mary; and their 12 children had settled in what became Marion County, he built a distillery and sold his first barrel of whiskey in 1795, calling it Old Jake Beam.

Beam not only started a distillery in a region of the commonwealth that grew rich with them, but he also started a line of whiskey makers that has stretched to an eighth generation. Jacob's son David joined the business and assumed the helm on his father's death, around 1818. David's son David M. Beam moved the distillery near Bardstown in the early 1850s. David M.'s son James Beauregard Beam took over in 1888 and moved the distillery again to sit closer to the newly built railroad line. Family and friends called James Beauregard "Jim," and the whiskey in the square bottle with a white label that still bears his name has become the best-selling Bourbon brand in the world.

Jim Beam's son T. Jeremiah ("Jere") joined him at the Clear Springs Distilling Company, as it was called, in 1913. The Bourbon brands made there consisted of Jefferson Club, Jim Beam, Old Tub, and Pebble-Ford.

Then Prohibition came, and Clear Springs went out of business.

After Repeal, Jim Beam persuaded a group of investors from Chicago to buy the site of the Murphy, Barber & Company distillery at Clermont. When the industry dried up, all of its buildings, except one warehouse, had been razed. The consortium of investors built a new distillery at the base of tree-covered hills overlooking wooded countryside, and in 1935, Jim Beam, now 71 years old, was making Bourbon again—though not as a distillery owner.

Jere Beam took the reins in 1944, and his father died three years later. Margaret, one of his sisters, married Frederick Booker Noe, and their son Booker, a grandson of Jim Beam, became the sixth generation in the Beam distilling line. A six-foot-four bear of a man, Booker ran the Jim Beam Distilling Company's second plant at Boston, Kentucky, a few miles west of Clermont, for almost four decades. He often took whiskey from a small selection of barrels that he deemed especially fine, blended them, and bottled the blend without filtering, at barrel strength, for his own enjoyment.

In 1987, Barry Berish, CEO of Beam, asked Booker to bottle something exceptional as gifts for special accounts. Not wanting to use regular Jim Beam bottles, Booker found empty wine bottles in a Beam warehouse. He filled them, applied a handwritten label on each, and shipped them to company headquarters.

The lucky recipients loved it and asked for more. In 1988—as a result of the demand from accounts and just as the Bourbon industry was seeing growth for the first time in decades—Beam launched Booker's, a premium whiskey in just 6,000 bottles. In 1992, building on that success, the company introduced the Small Batch Bourbon Collection, in which three more premium expressions joined Booker's: Basil Hayden, Baker's, and Knob Creek.

Even after Booker retired from active distilling, he traveled the world to lead tastings of the Small Batch Collection and charm audiences with accounts of his nondistilling activities, such as making beaten biscuits with the specialized tabletop machine inherited from his grandmother, curing his own country hams, and relaxing with good friend Jimmy Russell, Wild Turkey's master distiller. Booker's travel and interactions with the public helped shape the phenomenon of master distillers as the faces of their brands. Booker's son and grandson, Frederick Booker Noe (Fred) III

and (Freddie) IV have assumed that role, but it didn't always look like that would happen.

Fred Noe recalls that, when he was in high school in the 1970s, his father had been very frank with him about the future of the Bourbon industry: "Booker said, 'Don't bet on this! Been here, boy.' He had closed one of the [Beam] distilleries in the seventies. No one was drinking Bourbon." Asked what he might have done had Bourbon not staged a comeback, Fred Noe knew immediately. "I would have been a truck driver!" As a little boy, he had loved riding in the big trucks transporting barrels and cases of whiskey around the distillery. But Bourbon's popularity did rise again of course, and Fred Noe became the next Beam descendent to become a distiller in the family business.

Freddie Noe, when asked the same career question, had a ready answer, too: "Something culinary." The younger Noe has become renowned in his family as a cook. "My meatloaf is a favorite." Will there be a

ninth generation of distillers in the family? "My teenaged daughter is already telling me that she's going to be a great distiller," he replies.

Freddie Noe spends much of his time in the Fred B. Noe Distillery, a small (by Beam standards) facility with a capacity to make 1.2 million gallons of whiskey per year. (The main Clermont distillery produces about 26.5 million gallons annually.) Here, Freddie experiments with mash bills and fermentation techniques. He also creates his line of limited-release Little Book whiskeys—some of them strictly Kentucky creations; and others, blends in collaboration with parent company Suntory's Japanese and Canadian whiskys. The Fred B. Noe Distillery also gives rise to many of the expressions in the high-end Small Batch Collection.

The Clermont facility offers a choice of tours, including a short tasting experience, a look at different stages of production, and a longer, high-end VIP tour with many peeks behind the scenes. Another

good reason to visit is the distillery's full-service restaurant, the Kitchen Table, named for the round oak table in the Beam-Noe family house on North Third Street in Bardstown. (Originally Jim Beam's house, it became Booker Noe's home and now Fred Noe's, where, like his father, he hosts a backyard barbecue during the annual Kentucky Bourbon Festival.) In addition to a full bar offering all the Beam whiskeys, highballs on draft, and craft cocktails, the Kitchen Table menu features dishes made with locally sourced fare, including fried catfish, duck (sometimes venison) poppers, pulled pork barbecue, and pizzas with dough made from the same yeast strain used to make the distillery's Bourbons. Jim Beam captured that strain from the air in his Bardstown backyard when he returned to distilling after Prohibition.

The visitor center, called the American Outpost, contains the gift shop and tasting rooms. Built to look like a still house, it has a circular elevator to evoke the experience of riding up and down through a col-

umn still. It's a good place to pick up some of Beam's limited-edition whiskeys.

Nearby attractions include the defunct Chapeze Distillery and Bernheim Forest. Before reaching the distillery from I-65, along KY 245, turn left at the Forest Edge Winery. A short drive down Chapeze Lane leads to the abandoned Chapeze Distillery, which closed in 1965. Beam now owns the property and uses the warehouses. The 1981 movie *Stripes*, starring Bill Murray and John Candy, used the green, half-timbered house by the railroad track, once the distillery office, as its Eastern European outpost.

Directly across the highway from the distillery stands Bernheim Forest. The 16,000-acre site features an 800-acre arboretum designed by Olmsted Associates and planted with more than 8,000 varieties of trees, shrubs, and perennials. More than 40 miles of hiking trails crisscross the property. Isaac W. Bernheim—a German immigrant who arrived in America at age 18 with only $4 to his name and who made a fortune as a Bourbon distiller—gave the land to the people of Kentucky in gratitude for his professional success. Diageo makes his brand, I. W. Harper, today.

JAMES B. BEAM INSTITUTE FOR KENTUCKY SPIRITS

Beam Suntory, the parent company of Beam and Maker's Mark, helped found the James. B. Beam Institute within the University of Kentucky's College of Agriculture, Food, and Environment in 2019. It aims to *"lead the global advancement of the American whiskey industry through workforce education, scientific discovery, environmental sustainability, community, and social responsibility."* The facilities include *a teaching and research distillery with a 30-foot column still and its own rickhouse. The curriculum prepares students for careers in the spirits industry, with classes on distillation (chemistry, engineering), managing a distillery (business, law) and sustainability (food science, forestry, horticulture, entomology). Each March, the Institute hosts a conference with presentations on distilling techniques, maturation, marketing, and sustainability.*

TO MY FAMILY, PAST, PRESENT & FUTURE

▲ Fred and Freddie Noe, the current generations of the Beam distilling line, carrying on the family business.

Recommended Bottles

BARGAIN
Jim Beam White Label
Jim Beam Black Label
Old Grand Dad Bottled-in-Bond

VALUE
Basil Hayden Toast
Old Grand Dad 114

SPECIAL OCCASION
Knob Creek 12 Year
Booker's

SPLURGE
Little Book (various releases called "Chapters")

Tasting Notes

Beam uses two mash bills, most likely: 75 percent corn, 13 percent rye, 12 percent malted barley; and 63 percent corn, 27 percent rye, 10 percent malted barley. (The company neither confirms nor denies.) Basil Hayden and Old Grand Dad expressions use the mash bill with more rye. All others use the one with less rye. The distillery produces a multitude of brands, so flavor profiles can vary due to many factors, including distillate proof, barrel-entry proof, and barrel position in the warehouses. Temperatures can vary as much as 35°F from the top floor to the bottom of a seven-story warehouse, and alcohol evaporates faster on the higher, hotter floors. Bourbons meant to age for longer than four to five years typically sit on the middle or lower floors. Booker's releases three or four times per year, the releases designated as "Batches." Freddie Noe's Little Book releases, at no set times, as "Chapters."

JIM BEAM WHITE LABEL
40% ABV (80 proof)

Price and approachability have helped make this bottle the best-selling Bourbon in the world. Balanced with light brown sugar, vanilla, apples, and a touch of cinnamon and honey, it tastes light on the palate, making it ideal for a highball.

JIM BEAM BLACK LABEL
7 years old, 43% ABV (86 proof)

Aged longer than the White Label and bottled at higher proof, this expression has a bit more oomph. You'll find caramel corn, ripe apple, and a touch of licorice with cinnamon that changes to black pepper on the finish. Sip it neat or in a cocktail.

BASIL HAYDEN TOAST
40% ABV (80 proof)

Aromas include brown sugar, warm madeleines, and ripe apple. Expect a richer mouthfeel than regular Basil Hayden and flavors of vanilla and some cinnamon sugar on the palate and a touch of oak at the finish.

OLD GRAND DAD 114
57% ABV (114 proof)

It smells complex with vanilla, a pinch of cocoa powder, dates, orange peel, and cherry. It drinks very rich, almost chewy, with dried apricots, leather, and tobacco on the palate. Water releases more orange peel. It makes a marvelous pairing with dark chocolate.

KNOB CREEK 12 YEAR OLD
50% ABV (100 proof)

Expect loads of chewy saddle leather and roasted nuts. It feels rich and oily on the tongue. It features quite a bit of oak balanced nicely with some vanilla, toasted marshmallow, and dark fruit.

BOOKER'S STORYTELLER BATCH, 2023–04
7 years, 2 months, 29 days; 63.9% ABV (127.8 proof), all releases barrel-strength, usually 62.5 to 67.5% ABV (125 to 135 proof)

It evokes toasted nuts, caramel, and vanilla, like crème brûlée topped with chopped pecans. Some sweet oak accompanies a blend of cinnamon and white pepper.

LITTLE BOOK CHAPTER 7
59.1% ABV (118.1 proof)

It features lots of caramel on the nose with some figs, baking spices, and dried black currants, which carry to the palate, where winelike fruit and roasted nuts join them. Very smooth for the proof.

Heaven Hill Distillery

Founded in 1935

HeavenHillDistillery.com
1311 Gilkey Run Road
Bardstown, KY 40004

In 1920, before Prohibition went into effect, more than 200 distilleries were operating in Kentucky. Just six remained after Repeal in December 1933. The federal government had licensed those six to store, sell, and eventually, when stocks ran low, distill medicinal whiskey. When manufacturing and selling alcohol once again became legal, making Bourbon became a golden business opportunity, even amid the Great Depression.

Max Shapira, a German Jewish immigrant, had begun as a peddler and grew his business into a small Kentucky chain of stores selling affordable clothing. When his five sons—David, Ed, Gary, George, and Mose—became adults, each took charge of a store, which, unlike many other businesses of the time, proved profitable. They also seized the opportunity that Repeal presented. In 1935, distiller Joe Beam approached Ed Shapira, proprietor of the Bardstown store, to invest in a new distillery. Shapira knew nothing about whiskey, but he knew that anyone in Central Kentucky named Beam certainly did. Shapira invited his brothers to join him.

Ed's son, Max, executive chairman of Heaven Hill, explains the Shapiras' strategy: "My dad and his brothers were all in their thirties when the company was founded. The industry was starting out at the same time, as there were hardly any functioning distilleries, no inventory left over from prior to 1919, so their view was that this was an exciting opportunity. They were young, curious, ambitious, and thought it would be exciting to be a part of this as investors. They knew there were huge risks, as the economic conditions in the mid-1930s were among the harshest of the Great Depression, but still to be a part of this would be a once-in-a-lifetime chance. I call the initial amount invested 'Private Equity 1935-style.' It was a bit of a wing and a prayer then."

The company purchased property for the new facility just outside Bardstown on land owned by William Heavenhill. Apparently a typo in the registration paperwork resulted in the bisection of his name. Beam supervised the plant and put his son Harry in charge of distilling. Two years later, Heaven Hill released its Bourbon Falls whiskey. Other investors hadn't fared as well in their other ventures as the Shapiras, so about the time that Bourbon Falls released, the Shapiras bought them out to become sole owners. They waited patiently, and two years later released a four-year-old expression, putting the distillery's name on it: Old Heaven Hill Bottled-in-Bond.

Throughout the middle of the 20th century, Heaven Hill enjoyed steady growth, with Beam distillers making the Bourbon. In 1946, Joe's son Harry handed the reins to his cousin, Earl Beam, who had worked at the Jim Beam Distillery. Earl introduced the Evan Williams brand, named for one of Kentucky's first commercial distillers. In 1960, Earl's son Parker joined his father and in 1975 became master distiller himself. He created Elijah Craig Small Batch Bourbon as a premium brand for the company.

In 1971, Max Shapira, who had been working on Wall Street, returned to Kentucky to lead the business started by his father and uncles. "I grew up in a

Elijah Craig, a Baptist preacher, worked as a farmer-distiller in what eventually became Kentucky. A widely circulated story identifies him as the first to use charred oak barrels to age Bourbon. According to lore, his barn burned down, and he assembled barrels from wood salvaged from the fire. A colorful tale but totally untrue. For centuries, coopers had been heating barrel staves to bend them, and merchants often charred the inside of barrels to reuse them without cross-contaminating flavors.

household in which I heard 'Bourbon talk' at breakfast, lunch, and dinner. It all sounded pretty exciting, even as a child. On top of that, the property where Heaven Hill was located, some several hundred acres, became a playground of sorts for me. How could one not be infatuated with all of this? I'm not sure that I was predestined to be involved in some way, as it could have just been part of my DNA." But shortly after Shapira assumed the presidency of the company, Bourbon sales suffered a steep decline, industry wide. Shapira responded by diversifying the portfolio with other spirits. The company grew and eventually became the largest privately held, family-owned liquor company in America.

In the early 1980s, Parker Beam's son Craig followed in his forefathers' footsteps and eventually rose to become master distiller himself. By the early 1990s, interest in Bourbon was rekindling, and Heaven Hill was standing on the leading edge of that growth. But then, tragedy struck.

On November 7, 1996, a strong thunderstorm hit Bardstown. Although never confirmed, lightning likely struck one of the hilltop rickhouses, which caught fire. High winds spread the fire to other warehouses. As barrels exploded, they released rivers of flaming Bourbon that flowed downhill and into the distillery, which burned to the ground. The company lost about 90,000 barrels (7.7 million gallons) of whiskey. The catastrophe easily could have ended Heaven Hill, but other Kentucky distilleries, including Jim Beam and Old Forester, offered to make Heaven Hill's Bourbons until the company could replace its distillery. They used the Heaven Hill mash bills and even the same yeast strain, which had survived the fire in a heavily insulated freezer.

In 1999, Heaven Hill purchased the Bernheim Distillery in Louisville, a state-of-the-art facility that Diageo had built in 1992. The London-based spirits giant subsequently decided to exit the Bourbon business—temporarily, it turns out (page 71)—which

gave Heaven Hill the opportunity to acquire a ready-made facility. Heaven Hill distilling still takes place in Louisville, but most of the warehouses, as well as the bottling and distribution facilities, lie in Bardstown.

The Bardstown campus includes the Heaven Hill Bourbon Experience, which opened in 2006. A museum, shop, and venue for tours and tastings, the Bourbon Experience includes a cocktail bar with a deck overlooking the Bardstown rickhouses. The facility also offers a bottle-your-own experience: Enjoy a tasting of premium whiskeys, choose one to draw from the barrel, bottle it, and affix a personalized label to the bottle.

Heaven Hill also helped launch the redevelopment of Louisville's historic Whiskey Row. In 2013, its Evan Williams Bourbon Experience opened on West Main Street. Unknown to the company when it bought the building, the facilities stand only a few hundred yards from Evan Williams's riverbank distillery from the early 1800s. The Evan Williams Bourbon Experience features a small pot still operated by artisanal distiller Jodie Filiatreau that produces one barrel of Bourbon per day. It's available for sale as the Square 6 brand only from the on-site shop.

In 2017, Parker Beam lost his battle with ALS, and Craig Beam resigned from the company. Denny Potter became Heaven Hill's sixth master distiller, the first not named Beam. Conor O'Driscoll succeeded Potter in 2019. A third generation of the Shapira family assumed leadership of Heaven Hill in 2022 when Kate Shapira Latts, Max Shapira's daughter, and her husband, Allan Latts, became copresidents of the company. Max Shapira remains involved as executive chairman.

Today, Heaven Hill has the second-largest holding of aging whiskey in America, second only to Beam. Its stocks are aging in more than 60 warehouses across seven sites in Louisville, Bardstown, and Nelson and Bullitt Counties. Each warehouse holds between 10,000 and 60,000 barrels. To meet growing demand, Heaven Hill built a new distillery north of its Bardstown campus, which started production in late 2024. Today it makes about 10 million gallons (150,000 barrels) per year, but in time that volume can increase to 30 million gallons, or 450,000 barrels.

Recommended Bottles

Heaven Hill has a large portfolio. Its flagships, Elijah Craig and Evan Williams, originated with Parker Beam, and the company releases both brands in several expressions that vary in proof and age. Heaven Hill produces more bottled-in-bond expressions than any other distillery and also makes Mellow Corn whiskey, Pikesville and Rittenhouse ryes, and Bernheim Original Wheat Whiskey. Sales from the annual releases of the Parker's Heritage Collection, which vary in age, proof, and other parameters, benefit ALS research.

BARGAIN
Evan Williams
Evan Williams 1783
Larceny
Old Fitzgerald

VALUE
Heaven Hill Bottled-in-Bond
Elijah Craig
Larceny Barrel Proof

SPECIAL OCCASION
Henry McKenna 10 Year Bottled-in-Bond
Elijah Craig Barrel Proof
Evan Williams Single Barrel

SPLURGE
Old Fitzgerald Bottled-in-Bond Decanter Edition
Parker Heritage Collection Annual Release
Grain to Glass Kentucky Straight Bourbon Whiskey
Grain to Glass Kentucky Straight Wheated Bourbon

Tasting Notes

EVAN WILLIAMS

78% corn, 10% rye, 12% malted barley; 43% ABV (86 proof)

Honey, vanilla, a bit of pear, a pinch of cinnamon, and even a pinch of cocoa mark the flavor profile of this versatile sipper that you can enjoy neat, with an ice cube, or in a cocktail.

LARCENY

68% corn, 20% wheat, 12% malted barley; 46% ABV (92 proof)

It has flavors of vanilla custard sprinkled with cinnamon and nutmeg and topped with roasted almonds. A very smooth, balanced, wheated Bourbon. The barrel strength, with proof varying on the release, dials up the flavors and adds some apples.

HEAVEN HILL BOTTLED-IN-BOND

78% corn, 10% rye, 12% malted barley; 50% ABV (100 proof)

It has a classic caramel-vanilla profile with oranges and a bit of plum. Nutmeg and allspice balance the fruit with just a hint of honey.

ELIJAH CRAIG

78% corn, 10% rye, 12% malted barley; 47% ABV (94 proof)

It offers dark brown sugar with peaches and a touch of cinnamon. Think: peach cobbler without tasting too sweet. The highly recommended barrel-proof releases suggest brown sugar changing to toffee with the fruit and spice amplified.

HENRY MCKENNA BOTTLED-IN-BOND

78% corn, 10% rye, 12% malted barley; 10 years old; 50% ABV (100 proof)

In 2019, this Bourbon won Best Whiskey in the World at the San Francisco International Spirits Competition, which made it frustratingly hard to find for a few years. It smells floral with caramel apple, saddle leather, and ripe peaches on the nose. With a little water, cherries and a bit of chocolate join those flavors on the palate.

OLD FITZGERALD BOTTLED-IN-BOND DECANTER EDITION

68% corn, 20% wheat, 12% malted barley; 50% ABV (100 proof); limited annual release

Complex layers of flavors include rich caramel with a medley of fruit: blackberry, orange, dark cherry, and apple peel. Baking spices, chocolate, and vanilla join those notes with a long, fruit-filled finish.

GRAIN TO GLASS KENTUCKY STRAIGHT WHEATED BOURBON

53% corn, 35% wheat, 13% malted barley; no age statement; 60.5% ABV (121 proof)

It smells very nutty: roasted almonds and walnuts with oak and cedar. Toasted wheat crackers and dark caramel, sorghum, and molasses emerge from the rich mouthfeel, drying to oak and pepper. Some pepper on the finish also provides balance.

A TALE OF TWO ACTORS

Born in Louisville, the son of a former slave who fought for the Union, Tom Bullock worked as a bartender, perfecting his craft in the mid-1890s at the Pendennis Club, a private establishment that became famous for his Old-Fashioned. About 1904, he moved to Missouri to tend bar at the St. Louis Country Club, and in 1917, he became the first Black person to write a cocktail book. George Herbert Walker—a financier and forefather to the presidents Bush—contributed the introduction to the book, indicating the strength of Bullock's social standing at the time.

More recently, George Harrison, an Evan Williams Bourbon Experience tour guide, spotted a mural of Bullock at a Louisville restaurant, which inspired him and a friend to craft a presentation about Bullock for Evan Williams visitors. About the same time, Louisville Tourism was planning a new series called the Unfiltered Truth Collection: Black Heritage in Louisville. "We were far ahead of everybody else," says Harrison, "and the big thing for me was to be involved in this because of the contributions of African Americans to . . . Louisville. When we started doing this, people didn't know about Tom Bullock."

Two days a week, Harrison dons a white shirt, black bow tie, and red waistcoat to step into the role of Tom Bullock, making his Old-Fashioned during his Ideal Bartender Experience presentation. "People seem to know that the Old-Fashioned is Louisville's official cocktail. Bullock's Old-Fashioned is a bit different than ones most people have had. It's simple, sugar, bitters, water, and I use Evan Williams Bottled-in-Bond." The garnish makes it unique: a lemon peel expressed into the drink and dropped into the glass. "Several people have told me that it's the best Old-Fashioned they've ever had," says Harrison.

Harrison is an educator turned actor. As a "resting" actor, Lynn House worked in Chicago restaurants between onstage performances. "I found myself really interested in what was happening in the spirit scene and was working at a fine dining restaurant. We sold really crappy cocktails. We had a great wine list and a great menu, but our cocktails were horrible. Everything glowed."

House explained to the owner that cocktail quality should match the excellence of the food and wine. He tasked her with upgrading the cocktails, so she learned everything she could about mixed drinks. She read cocktail books and completed the culinary mixology course at Southern Glazer's Wine and Spirits Academy.

Eventually, she moved to Blackbird, a Michelin-starred and James Beard Award–winning restaurant. Her drinks garnered attention, but pumping cocktail shakers gave her a repetitive strain injury in her right elbow. She needed a spirits job with fewer physical demands. Heaven Hill hired her as a national brand ambassador for Pama, the company's pomegranate liqueur. "Even though I was representing the one liquor, I started teaching myself about the rest of the portfolio. When we went into the market, I told our teams that I could train them on other spirits, too. After about two years, my bosses sat me down and said, 'You're already doing it, so we might as well give you a new title.'" That's how she became national brand educator and, now, national spirit specialist and portfolio mixologist.

Still based in Chicago, House travels the country, introducing people to Heaven Hill's products. "With cocktails, we make our whiskeys approachable to the novice drinker and to the experienced drinker. I served Elijah Craig in a cocktail this weekend, and it's 94 proof. People enjoyed it who didn't think they could drink a 94-proof whiskey." House's mother and grandmother both enjoyed Bourbon, so she has another mission as an educator. "It's a passion of mine, when on the road and doing cocktails, to dispel those myths that women like only flavored whiskey."

Stitzel-Weller Distillery

Founded in 1935

StitzelWellerDistillery.com
3860 Fitzgerald Road
Louisville, KY 40216

On May 4, 1935—a gray, drizzly Saturday—Omaha won the Kentucky Derby. The three-year-old colt made racing history later that year when he won the Preakness and Belmont, becoming only the third horse to earn the Triple Crown. But on that same gray Saturday, Bourbon history happened, too. The Stitzel-Weller Distillery opened in Louisville.

An owner of the new distillery, Julian "Pappy" Van Winkle had started his Bourbon career as a salesman for whiskey wholesaler W. L. Weller & Sons, which sourced much of its product from the Arthur Philip Stitzel Distillery. Van Winkle and fellow employee

Alex T. Farnsley eventually bought a controlling interest in Weller, and shortly after Prohibition ended, Van Winkle, Farnsley, and Stitzel merged their companies to form this new enterprise.

Van Winkle decided to make its Bourbon using wheat as the secondary grain, rather than the usual rye. Virtually all wheated Bourbons today owe their mash bills to Van Winkle's innovation. On the distillery's cooling tower, "Old Fitzgerald," the name of Stitzel-Weller's flagship brand, still remains visible in the patterned bricks. (Heaven Hill now owns and makes the brand, still a wheated Bourbon.) Other brands included Weller, distilled at Buffalo Trace, and Rebel Yell, remade as Rebel and now a Lux Row product. Van Winkle insisted on bottling all his Bourbons at 50 percent ABV (100 proof). His mantra: "Why pay for water?" Consumers could adjust the proof as they liked, rather than buying whiskey diluted by the distillery.

With the decline of Bourbon in the 1960s, Stitzel-Weller's fortunes took a downturn as well, and the company's shareholders forced Julian Van Winkle Jr., who had taken over after his father's retirement, to sell. United Distillers, now Diageo, eventually acquired the property, which it used for its warehouses and to make its Bulleit whiskeys until building the Bulleit Distillery in Shelby County (page 71). Today, Stitzel-Weller also serves as the home for other American whiskeys in the Diageo portfolio.

Exhibits at the facility's museum explain the history of the place and the influences of Van Winkle and Isaac W. Bernheim, whose eponymous distillery stood on nearby Bernheim Lane. Modeled after Monticello, Thomas Jefferson's home, the museum building contained Van Winkle's office. The tour showcases the experimental still, rickhouses where I. W. Harper and Blade and Bow age, and the old Stitzel-Weller barrel repair shop. (Bernheim named his Bourbon "Harper," after an associate, perhaps believing that a less Jewish-sounding name would sell better.)

THE GARDEN AND GUN CLUB

Richly appointed in leather and wood, this luxurious lounge—decorated with hunting prints and a collaboration with *Garden & Gun* magazine—offers an array of spirits from the Diageo portfolio, curated cocktails, and small plates. The menu features flights of limited-edition Bourbons and individual pours of the more expensive whiskeys, so you can enjoy the rarer expressions without having to invest in a whole bottle.

Recommended Bottles

VALUE
I. W. Harper Cabernet Cask Reserve
Blade and Bow

SPECIAL OCCASION
I. W. Harper 15 Year Old

SPLURGE
Orphan Barrel Releases, 14 to 23 years old

Tasting Notes

I. W. HARPER CABERNET CASK RESERVE

73% corn, 18% rye, 9% malted barley; 4 years old before finishing in ex-Cabernet barrels; 45% ABV (90 proof)
Just enough wine from the finishing barrels creates interest and some fruit without masking the whiskey. It tastes very caramel forward with some blackberries and chocolate-covered cherries.

BLADE AND BOW

mash bill not released, no age statement, 45.5% ABV (91 proof)
This brand ages with the Solera method, borrowed from Sherry making, in which some younger Bourbon goes into barrels of already aged whiskey, some of which goes into even older barrels, and so on, creating a stable house style. Expect ripe apples, pear, rich vanilla, and a generous pinch of baking spices on the nose and palate. Nuts and a pinch of anise add complexity before ending in a bit of sweet oak.

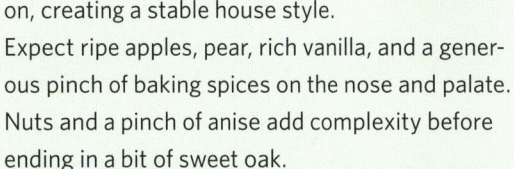

I. W. HARPER 15 YEAR OLD

73% corn, 18% rye, 9% malted barley; 15 years old; 43% ABV (86 proof)
Waves of vanilla roll from the glass, followed by cherries. Think: amaretto. The palate adds caramel and sweet oak and a long, warming finish.

Willett Distillery

Founded in 1936

WillettDistillery.com
1869 Loretto Road
Bardstown, KY 40004

In 1935, Lambert Willett bought a wooded property on a hill overlooking Heaven Hill's warehouses south of Bardstown. His sons, Johnny and A. L. "Thompson" Willett, built and ran the distillery on the site. The small operation produced about 50 barrels a day of Old Bardstown Bourbon. During the economic downturn of the 1970s, they couldn't sell enough Bourbon to stay in business, so Willett shuttered in 1981. But it didn't stay that way.

Thompson Willett's daughter Martha and her husband, Norwegian immigrant Even Kulsveen, reopened it in 1984, creating a line of carefully sourced, small-batch Bourbons. The Kulsveens gradually added more buildings to the site, expanding the distillery, which remains family owned and operated today. Their son Drew serves as master distiller; Drew's wife, Janelle, manages the visitor center; and their daughter Britt works as company president.

Willett's 1,200-gallon Vendome copper pot still shines as a centerpiece of the distillery tour. "My father designed it," says Drew Kulsveen. "We hold a patent on it." Kulsveen uses the pot still—with its squat base and long, thin neck—as his doubler. After the distillate comes off the unusually slender, 24-inch-diameter column still, it goes into the pot still, resulting in smooth, floral whiskeys. "The unique shape contributes to our flavor profile. How stills are shaped can affect flavor, creating different congeners and different levels of those congeners, from heavy to light."

If you've visited the bigger legacy distilleries, this hilltop collection of seven original rickhouses—640 feet above sea level, the highest in central Kentucky—

may feel almost miniature. Each holds only 5,000 barrels, about a tenth of most seven-story rickhouses. Addressing demand, Willett added a warehouse with a 25,000-barrel capacity in 2020 and plans to increase production capacity dramatically in 2025 with a second distillery and new warehouses in Springfield. "The Bardstown capacity is about 25,000 barrels per year," says Drew Kulsveen. "Springfield will be able to produce 60,000 barrels annually. We're going to be very busy."

THE BAR AT WILLETT

On the second floor of the visitor center, this comfortable space with a working stone fireplace has an open kitchen where you can watch kitchen staff preparing fine lunches. Drawing on local and international flavors, the small plates range from snacks with drinks to substantial meals. Longtime features include olives seasoned with crumbled walnuts and orange zest, an egg salad sandwich made with smoked mayonnaise, and pâté en croute served with Dijon mustard and pistachios. The bar has its own ice program and serves many of the cocktails with one large crystal-clear cube stamped with the Willett family crest. In good weather, sit on the balcony overlooking the wooded grounds.

▲ On the distillery tour, keep an eye out for the working cats that patrol the buildings, each with its own territory, and don't be surprised if one walks by a tour group with a mouse in its mouth.

Recommended Bottles

BARGAIN
Old Bardstown Bottled-in-Bond

VALUE
Johnny Drum Private Stock
Kentucky Vintage
Pure Aged XO

SPECIAL OCCASION
Noah's Mill
Rowan's Creek
Willett Pot Still Reserve

Tasting Notes

Willett doesn't disclose mash bills or give age statements for its Bourbons, but by law, anything bottled-in-bond must have aged for at least four years. The Willett Family Estate Bourbon is available only as single-barrel bottles or private selections for restaurants and retailers. Each bottling features unique ages and proofs. Check the menu of a fine whiskey bar to taste one.

OLD BARDSTOWN BOTTLED-IN-BOND
50% ABV (100 proof)

Cherries dominate the nose and palate, like the best cherry turnover with vanilla icing. Generous caramel and oak keep it from tasting too sweet.

JOHNNY DRUM PRIVATE STOCK
50.5% ABV (101 proof)

This bottle elegantly merges vanilla, apple, and sweet oak with a dusting of cinnamon sugar. It's very easy to sip, even at triple-digit proof. It sometimes disappears from retail shelves for some time. When available, carpe diem.

KENTUCKY VINTAGE
45% ABV (90 proof)

It evokes warm, roasted nuts with dates, vanilla pudding, and a bit of apple blossom. The long finish ends with a flourish of peppery spice and oak. It makes an excellent base for just about any Bourbon cocktail.

WILLETT POT STILL RESERVE

The glass bottles, 750 milliliters or 1.75 liters, commemorate Even Kulsveen's patented still design, making it easy to spot on store or bar shelves. It has aromas of lemon tart with a shortbread crust. The palate exhibits an impressive balance of caramel, vanilla, citrus, floral notes, and sweet oak, all of which fade in tandem during the long finish.

Maker's Mark Distillery

Founded in 1953

MakersMark.com
3350 Burks Spring Road
Loretto, KY 40037

In 1805, Charles Burks built Burks Spring Distillery, which he ran until his death in 1861. His family operated it until Prohibition, when it closed. The still was removed, but the frame buildings and farmland remained. Bill and Marge Samuels purchased the property in 1953 and renamed it Star Hill Farm. After Prohibition, Samuels had managed the T. W. Samuels Distillery outside Bardstown, named after his great-grandfather, but the family no longer owned it. Samuels didn't love the Bourbon produced there and wanted to make his own: a smooth Bourbon to counter the rough-and-tumble reputation of American whiskey. After consulting with Julian "Pappy" Van Winkle, Samuels used wheat, rather than the spicier rye, in his mash bill. (All the Van Winkle brands from the Stitzel-Weller distillery in Louisville, including Old Fitzgerald, used wheat instead of rye.)

Marge coined the name Maker's Mark and created the signature bottle design with the red wax on the neck and the star with a Roman numeral representing the number of generations of Bourbon makers in the family. The name came from her passion for collecting fine pewter, each piece stamped with the mark of its maker. For the wax seal, she took inspiration from Cognac producers, who used that technique to prevent corks from drying out or leaking. With the deep fryer in her kitchen, she experimented with wax formulas until she found the right one for the job. She also wanted visitors to be able to see for themselves where and how the picturesque distillery made the liquid. In short, Marge Samu-

▲ Bill and Marge Samuels

els single-handedly made the Maker's Mark brand instantly recognizable and all but invented modern Bourbon tourism.

In the 1960s and '70s, much of the spirits industry declined worldwide, but Bill Samuels Jr. bucked that trend. Scottish producers, experiencing the same downturn in sales, rolled out the marketing strategy of labeling its single malts as "premium." In 1965, he tasked Doe-Anderson, the company's Louisville ad agency, with creating a tagline to promote Maker's Mark as premium, too. The result: "It tastes expensive . . . and is." The Bourbon retailed for less than $20 at the time, though, and still sells for a modest sum, considering the number of bottles that go for $50, $100, or more. Consumers took notice, and Maker's Mark sales rebounded, lifting the category with it.

For almost four decades, Samuels Jr. served as the face of the brand. Outgoing and outspoken, he sported flamboyant outfits, sometimes appearing in full-color print ads. In one, he wore his riding kit while standing next to a horse, its tail facing the camera. The caption: "Here I am with my not-so-famous racehorse Diller. (That's me on the left.)"

As the market recovered, major distilleries resuscitated or developed brands that multinational conglomerates assembled into massive portfolios. But Maker's stayed the course with its original 90-proof expression. In 2010, as Samuels Jr. was about to step

> Parent company Suntory Global Spirits ships used Maker's barrels to Scotland, where Laphroaig ages in them.

down as CEO, he decided that he wanted a signature whiskey as part of his legacy. Enter Maker's 46.

Samuels worked with coopers at Independent Stave Company to find a recipe for seared oak staves to immerse in barrels of Maker's during extra aging to create new flavors. The number comes from the number of the stave recipe—not the 46th stave tried, as commonly believed. This signature whiskey evolved into the limited annual releases of the Wood Finishing Series.

Beth Buckner, senior manager of innovation and blending, oversees that series, which formally began in 2019. These annual or biannual releases allow for variation on stave treatment beyond those used for the Private Barrel Selections (page 69). Past releases include an extra-aged 12-year, which spent four years in the cellar and comes from barrels from two dif-

> With special labels and different colors of wax, commemorative bottles celebrate special occasions, such as blue wax in 2012, when the University of Kentucky won the NCAA basketball championship, and a 2023 label depicting Marge Samuels to mark the opening of the gallery dedicated to her.

ferent floors of a rickhouse. Warehouse placement matters, and Maker's stands apart as the only major distillery that rotates barrels to different floors during aging. But the extra-aged 12-year barrels stayed in place. According to Buckner, "The Wood Finishing Series program uses one stave, or I shouldn't say 'one' stave because, in 2020, we used two: SE and pr5. But it's meant to stand on its own, a complete product. Private Select is composed of five staves to be used together, and 46 will always be in the program and can stand on its own. The others enhance the flavors and push boundaries, but they blend together to make the finished product."

At the distillery, you can choose from a variety of tours. The basic, one-hour excursion winds through the still house, where an antique press prints the labels; the gallery honoring Marge Samuels and her pewter collection; the cellar; and, of course, a tast-

THE SAMUELS HOUSE

Robert Samuels, the first whiskey-maker in the family, fought with Commander George Washington in the American war of independence. After the war, Robert moved his family, including son John, and his 60-gallon copper pot still to central Kentucky. In 2020, Rob Samuels purchased the two-story, red-brick Georgian house built near Bardstown circa 1820 by John Samuels, one of his quintuple-great uncles.

Rob Samuels restored the ancestral home as a showcase for the family's distilling legacy, and it also serves as a luxurious three-bedroom space that guests can rent for a getaway. The house features original woodwork, hand-painted murals, vintage furnishings, and state-of-the-art bathrooms. The parlor contains displays of historic Maker's bottles and the deep fryer that Marge Samuels famously used to create the signature red sealing wax. Visit TheSamuelsHouse.com for more information.

ing room. You also can dip a bottle in the famous red wax before buying it. Art lovers can take the Art and Design Tour, which highlights more than 20 original works displayed in a gallery and throughout the grounds. Artists include Gordon Browning, Dale Chihuly, Roman Feral, and Thomas Vieth. Chihuly, an internationally renowned and award-winning glass artist, created an intricate, amber sculpture suspended from the ceiling of the gallery as well as *The Spirit of the Maker*, a 1,300-piece, 6-by-40-foot warehouse installation showcased on the basic tour. The colors of the work reference different components of Bourbon: blue for water, red for red winter wheat, and yellow for corn. Among the abstract shapes, look closely for four cherubs that represent the "angels' share" of whiskey that evaporates during aging. Other special tours include a farm tour, an oak-

tree tour that may include planting a seedling, and an extended tour that visits the property's nature preserve with hiking trails, spring-fed lakes, and farm. Seasonal experiences also highlight the restaurant and cocktail bar.

The 1,100-acre campus features a white oak nursery, truffle farm, organic heirloom vegetable garden, contemporary art gallery, and more. The US Department of the Interior designated Star Hill Farm a National Historic Landmark, and the company ranks as the world's largest B-corporation distillery. That last designation and Regenified certification reflect Maker's commitment to sustainability and responsible land management. Why so many special attractions and initiatives? "Our vision for the distillery and the farm is to become the most culturally rich, endearing, and environmentally responsible home

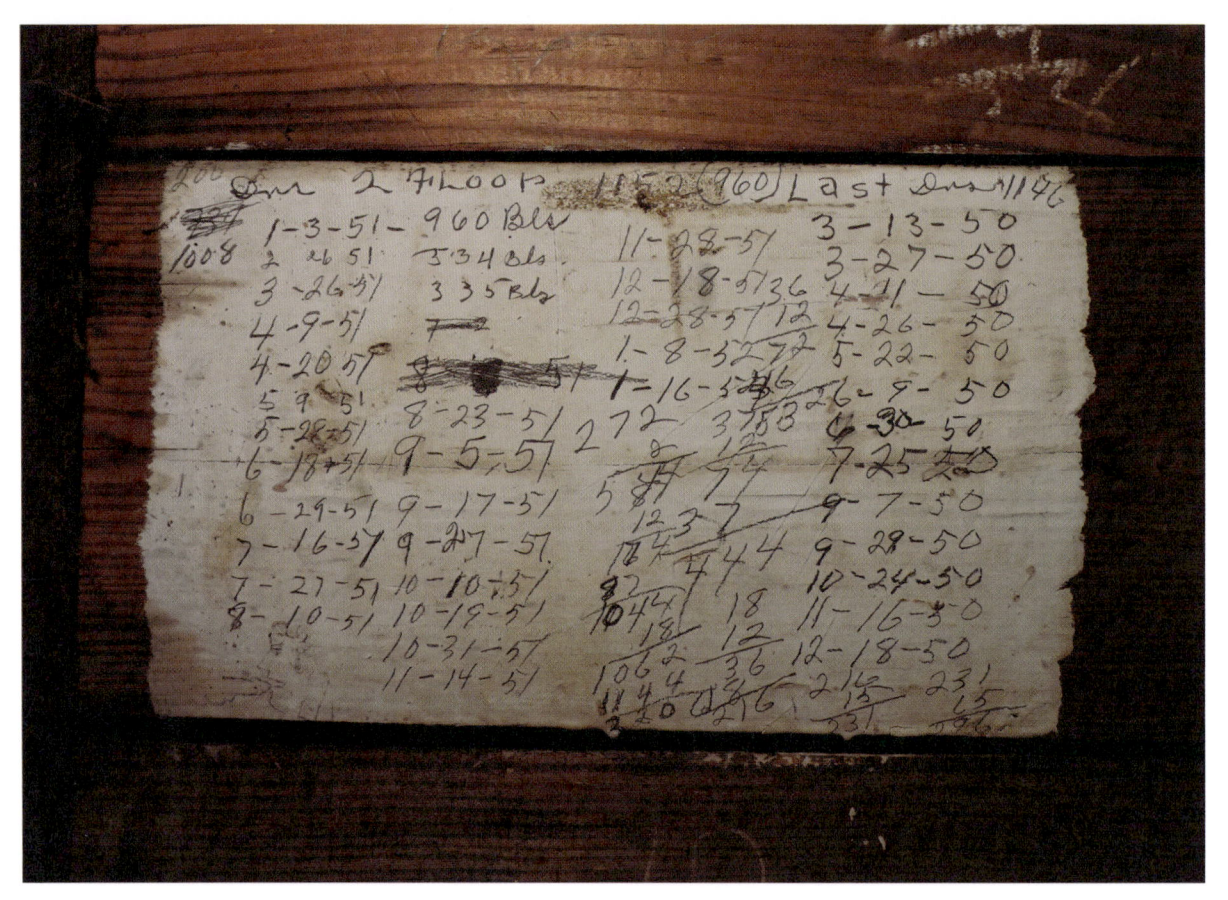

▲ Date calculations from an old rickhouse.

place of any brand in the world," says Rob Samuels, the managing director. In 2011, he took the reins from his father, Samuels Jr., emphasizing the visitor experience, a vision that began with Marge Samuels, his grandmother.

Amanda Humphrey came from London to help with the cocktail program, but her duties soon expanded. Now the advocacy and experience manager, she has a prominent role in many of the special attractions. "What we're really trying to carve out is the education-inspiration piece and how we bring people into the farm experiences across the 1,100 acres. They ask, 'What's the working farm got to do with Bourbon?' Bourbon is an agricultural product; it's nature distilled. If we're not good stewards of our land, then we're not going to be able to make whiskey in 200 years' time."

▲ Advocacy and experience manager Amanda Humphrey with the distillery's resident truffle dog, Star

Humphrey also handles Star, the resident truffle dog. A Lagotto Romagnolo, he has an incredibly keen sense of smell, capable of detecting the fungal delicacy growing underground on tree roots. The honey, sorghum, and truffles harvested on the property go into custom cocktails served at the distillery's cocktail bar. Star Hill Provisions, the restaurant, also works closely with all aspects of the property, serving heirloom vegetables from the kitchen garden, lamb samosas sourced from the sheep used to trim the meadows, and hamburgers from the herd of Wagyu cattle.

Elsewhere on the property, a solar array powers all the rickhouses, with excess power sold to the local grid. A glass recycling program transforms empty bottles into sand used for hiking trails and given to Marion County for road maintenance. The white oak nursery strategically contributes to the White Oak Genetics and Genomics Research Program run by the Department of Forestry and Natural Resources at the University of Kentucky. All these initiatives highlight the company's commitment to sustainability.

For the future, Rob Samuels hints at plans to include lodgings. "One of our aspirations is to become a Relais & Château destination, like Blackberry Farm in Tennessee or Old Edwards Inn in Highlands, North Carolina, where you have this really personal spirit of hospitality and local culinary dining."

Recommended Bottles

BARGAIN
Maker's Mark

VALUE
Maker's Mark Cask Strength
Maker's 46

SPECIAL OCCASION
Maker's Mark Private Barrel Selections

▲ Rob Samuels beneath the Dale Chihuly glass installation in the warehouse.

Tasting Notes

The mash bill for all expressions of Maker's Mark contains 70 percent, 16 percent red winter wheat, 14 percent malted barley. Barrel-entry proof sits at 110 (55 percent ABV), and a standard batch consists of 378 barrels that hold five- to seven-year-old Bourbon.

MAKER'S MARK

45% ABV (90 proof)
Light caramel and distinct vanilla accompany notes of apple, berries, pecans, and just the right touch of oak for balance. Sweet oak lingers in the finish. It makes an exceptional Old-Fashioned.

MAKER'S 46

47% ABV (94 proof)
It begins with big-time vanilla, the first aroma to rise from the glass. It still exhibits apple and berries, but it tastes sweeter than the 90 proof, with a longer, more peppery finish. Try it in a Manhattan.

MAKER'S MARK CASK STRENGTH

54 to 57% ABV (108 to 114 proof)
It evokes ripe apples, vanilla, honey, and oak. Depending on the batch, you may detect a sweet hint of smoke. Add a splash of water or an ice cube to release more apple and honey.

MAKER'S MARK PRIVATE BARREL SELECTIONS

55.5 to 57% ABV (111 to 114 proof)
Secondary aging uses five different, custom-toasted staves. The selector can choose from a combination of 10 staves: 10 of any one stave, two each of all five, or some combination in between . . . for 1,001 possible combinations! The staves have holes in one end, through which a steel ring threads to suspend them in a barrel of Bourbon that already has aged the usual five to seven years. The barrel spends nine additional weeks in the hillside limestone cellar at a constant temperature of 50°F so the liquid absorbs flavors primarily from the suspended staves rather than the barrel. Many restaurants and retailers, domestic and abroad, feature their own selections on shelves and in bars. The staves impart the following flavors.

- **Baked American Pure 2**: American oak toasted slowly at a low temperature in a convection oven; caramel, brown sugar, vanilla, milk chocolate, cinnamon.
- **Maker's 46**: French oak seared with infrared heat; sweet baking spices, dried cherries, sweet pipe tobacco, vanilla.
- **Roasted French Mendiant**: French oak cooked in a low-temperature convection oven; dried dark fruit, milk chocolate, nuts.
- **Seared French Cuvee**: French oak seared with infrared heat, ridged staves; caramel and toasted oak.
- **Toasted French Spice**: French oak toasted in a convection oven, first on high heat, then low; a little smoke, rich vanilla, some citrus, and baking spices.

Bulleit Distilling Company

Founded in 1987

Bulleit.com
3464 Benson Pike
Shelbyville, KY 40065

In 1987, Lexington attorney Tom Bulleit started a Bourbon brand based on a great-great-grandfather's 19th-century recipe. Not a distiller himself, Bulleit had his Bourbon contract-distilled at today's Buffalo Trace Distillery in Frankfort (page 3). A decade later, he sold the brand to Seagram, which moved production to Four Roses in Lawrenceburg (page 21).

In 1992, beverage giant Diageo, then called United Distillers, had built the Bernheim Distillery, a state-of-the-art plant in Louisville. But toward the end of that decade, the company concluded that Bourbon didn't look like a growth category for the firm. In 1999, it sold Bernheim to Heaven Hill, which hadn't had its own facility to make whiskey since the catastrophic fire of 1996 (page 47). In 2000, Diageo bought several Seagram brands, including Bulleit. The largest liquor company in the world once again had a Bourbon, but not a dedicated Bourbon distillery. The Four Roses brand was growing, so that facility couldn't keep making Bulleit in Lawrenceburg. Diageo contracted production of Bulleit to various American distilleries.

Seeing that Bourbon was going somewhere after all, Diageo spent $115 million to build a new distillery. Constructed on nearly 500 acres in Shelby County, east of Louisville, the carbon-neutral, environmentally efficient facility opened in 2019. Diageo built much of the visitor center, which includes the cocktail bar and gift shop, into a hillside to minimize the need for heating and air conditioning. The site uses solar energy and sends zero waste to landfills. That commitment to sustainability doesn't detract from the visitor experience, though. The visitor center and tasting room feel both elegant and rustic. Barrels stack upright, floor to ceiling, in the central room, which features leather or upholstered armchairs and sofas. The signature orange of Bulleit's branding appears throughout the building.

The tour emphasizes flavors produced during fermentation and distillation. Distillery manager Courtney King has a favorite exercise for visitors. She passes around a small spray bottle of new-make whiskey, fresh off the still, urging everyone to spray a bit on their hands. "Take a whiff," she instructs. "You'll smell the aromatics we've extracted, some fruits and chocolate. Now clap and rub, and you start to get the raw material, almost like straight malt."

Bulleit's longtime doubler came from the Stitzel-Weller Distillery in Louisville (page 53), which Diageo also owns and uses to bottle Bulleit whiskeys. Of the doubler, which recently returned there, King said, "She's been distilling for quite some time, but she does make some pretty good distillate. She still rocks and rolls."

Recommended Bottles

Bulleit also makes a notable rye, historically sourced from MGP in Lawrenceburg, Indiana, and in 2024 released an American Single Malt made entirely from malted barley.

VALUE
Bulleit Bourbon
Bulleit Barrel Strength

SPECIAL OCCASION
Bulleit 10 Year Old

Tasting Notes

Bulleit Bourbons use a high-rye mash bill: 68 percent corn, 28 percent rye, 4 percent malted barley. The flagship and barrel-strength expressions don't carry age statements, but they can contain a blend of barrels that have aged from five to eight years.

BULLEIT BOURBON
45% ABV (90 proof)
Caramel and vanilla with candied nuts, some pears, and apple characterize the nose. Medium bodied, it tastes complex with almonds, cinnamon, and some oak joining flavors previewed by its aromas. The long finish features baking spices.

BULLEIT BARREL STRENGTH
60% ABV (120 proof) (varies by batch)
Expect lightly floral aromas and a touch of mint with rich banana pudding and flavors of caramel, baking spices, and mixed berries. The long finish tastes impressively smooth for its hefty proof.

BULLEIT 10 YEAR OLD
45.6% ABV (91.2 proof)
Floral aromas pair with vanilla and spiced fruit, such as dried apricots and cherries. A rich mouthfeel amplifies intense flavors of marzipan, dark cherries, and crème brûlée. The long finish releases peppery spice and some oak.

Woodford Reserve Distillery

Founded in 1996

WoodfordReserve.com
7785 McCracken Pike
Versailles, KY 40383

In 1812, America declared war on Britain. That year in Kentucky, which had gained statehood 20 years earlier, Elijah Pepper built a distillery on the bank of Glenns Creek in Woodford County. The facility included a warehouse with a capacity of about 9,000 barrels. Pepper made well-regarded whiskey there until his death in 1838, when control passed to Oscar Pepper, his son.

The younger Pepper hired Scottish distiller James Crow, who may or may not have had a medical degree, as he claimed, from the University of Edinburgh. But Crow did have expertise in chemistry and receives credit for first applying scientific rigor to the production of American whiskey. Crow used a hydrometer to measure alcohol levels at various stages of distillation and aging, taking detailed notes throughout the process. He also receives credit for the first commercial application of the sour mash process in fermentation. As with making sourdough bread, a portion of the previous fermentation goes into the next batch to maintain consistency of flavor and to jump-start the fermentation process.

Under Crow's guidance, the Old Oscar Pepper Distillery produced Old Oscar Pepper and Old Crow Bourbons. The latter became so renowned that Henry Clay, the famous US senator from Kentucky, made it his whiskey of choice. During the Civil War, when President Abraham Lincoln heard complaints about

General Ulysses Grant's level of whiskey consumption, Lincoln reportedly replied, "What is the brand? I want it for all my generals." It was Old Crow.

The distillery eventually came under the control of Colonel E. H. Taylor Jr., who sold it to George T. Stagg in 1878 (page 3), but Stagg didn't keep it for long. He sold it to Leopold Labrot and James Graham, and it operated as Labrot & Graham until Prohibition forced it to close in 1918. Reopened later under different ownership, it came to Brown-Forman in 1940. For a few years, they produced whiskey here, called Kentucky Dew.

In the 1970s, Brown-Forman sold the facility, which, at the end of the decade, converted to making gasohol to help offset the international oil crisis. When the gas shortage eased, the site closed again. In the early 1990s, Owsley Brown II, a great-grandson of company founder George Garvin Brown, noted the growing success of such premium brands as Maker's Mark and Blanton's, and the importance of Maker's Mark's historic distillery site as a tourist destination. He advocated bringing it back into the portfolio, but at least one member of the board of directors objected, dubbing it "Owsley's Folly." But in 1994, Brown prevailed, and Brown-Forman repurchased the old distillery.

The company restored the 19th-century stone buildings, installed a trio of copper pot stills made

by Forsyths of Scotland, and built a visitor center. The location reopened in 1996 as the Labrot & Graham Distillery to produce premium brand Woodford Reserve. The name later changed to Woodford Reserve Distillery to avoid confusion about the brand name and place of origin. When it opened, Woodford Reserve was the only Kentucky Bourbon distillery using copper pot stills instead of column stills. It remains one of the few distilleries—along with parent company's Old Forester, Michter's, and Buffalo Trace—to use temperature-controlled warehouses.

When Brown-Forman reacquired Woodford Reserve, it planned to source all the corn from a Kentucky farm. The Brown family owned that first farm, but only briefly because the farmer retired within months. Then the distillery contacted Doug Langley in Shelby County, who has supplied all the corn milled, cooked, fermented, and distilled here ever since. His production has grown with the brand, first stored in three small silos that he replaced years ago with a complex of giant grain storage bins resembling a block of skyscrapers. Langley fondly recalls when, a few years ago, he made a private barrel selection of Woodford Reserve: "The corn left the farm as dry grain and came back as liquid whiskey. That was pretty neat."

When Woodford Reserve opened, Brown-Forman's master distiller was Lincoln Henderson. He used the same mash bill as the company's original brand, Old Forester: 72 percent corn, 18 percent rye, 10 percent malted barley. But a slightly higher proof made it more robust and complex, while still serving as an elegant sipping Bourbon. Under Henderson, Peggy Noe Stevens had trained to become the Bourbon industry's first woman master taster. As director of homeplace marketing, she assembled a team of culinary professionals—including chef-in-residence David Larson, who had owned the highly regarded Pampered Chef restaurant in Lexington—to emphasize the complex flavors of the new product.

In consultation with Henderson, Stevens and Larson worked with other Kentucky chefs—including James Beard Award nominees Ouita Michel, Anthony Lamas, and Jim Gerhardt—to identify hundreds of flavor notes and create the industry's first culinary flavor wheel, which appeared in *The Woodford Reserve Culinary Cocktail Tour*, published by Brown-Forman

in 2005. By then, Henderson had retired, and Chris Morris had become master distiller. Ouita Michel succeeded Larson as the distillery's chef. Morris and Michel further modified the flavor wheel and used it to promote the brand's profile. The distillery also broke ground by hosting lunches and dinners to highlight Bourbon pairings.

Morris introduced the Master's Collection, annual limited-edition releases, which feature bottlings using four grains instead of three or which age for additional time in ex-Chardonnay or ex–Pinot Noir barrels. He also created the popular Woodford Reserve Double Oak. "The Double Oaked barrel is crafted from oak that has seasoned for nine months. The interior of the barrel is toasted for 40 minutes

and then charred for 5 to 10 seconds. It's designed to highlight Woodford Reserve's sweet aromatic profile," says Morris. "It's finished according to taste but no less than 6 months and no longer than 12. The barrel isn't used again, so Double Oaked retains its Kentucky Straight Bourbon designation. The whiskey has never touched anything but new, charred oak."

In 2018, Woodford Reserve became the official Bourbon of the Kentucky Derby. For the Derby and Christmas, the company releases commemorative bottles with special labels commissioned from artists. Also each year, sales of limited-edition mint juleps in sterling silver cups with rare garnishes benefit thoroughbred-related charities.

Under Morris, other whiskey styles entered the distillery's portfolio, including Woodford Reserve Rye, Woodford Reserve Wheat Whiskey, and Woodford Reserve Malt. In 2023, he retired as master distiller, handing the reins to Elizabeth McCall, who became the first woman master distiller of a legacy Kentucky Bourbon distillery. McCall has continued Woodford's culinary tradition and especially enjoys exploring the flavors of Woodford Double Oaked. "Double Oaked had always been like a dessert Bourbon, so we were always doing dessert pairings. Then our brand ambassador at the time, Casey Gray, suggested doing events in February, around Valentine's Day, with chocolate." By 2024, those events led to a partnership with Compartés, a Los Angeles chocolatier, which produced a special box of four chocolates— butterscotch, pear nutmeg, oak-smoked salted caramel, and maple pecan—to amplify or contrast with the flavors in Double Oak.

The tour of the picturesque distillery, designated a National Historic Landmark, begins in the welcome center, which includes a bar featuring a Baccarat crystal chandelier and a deck overlooking pastureland dotted with grazing racehorses. A shuttle provides transportation downhill to the distillery buildings and back up to another building housing tasting rooms and retail shop, where, if you like, you can buy chocolates and, of course, bottles of Woodford Reserve.

Recommended Bottles

VALUE
Woodford Reserve Distiller's Select

SPECIAL OCCASION
Woodford Reserve Double Oaked

SPLURGE
Woodford Reserve Master's Collection

Tasting Notes

Woodford Reserve Bourbons have the same mash bill as Brown-Forman sibling Old Forester: 72 percent corn, 18 percent rye, 10 percent malted barley. Limited releases available only at the distillery include Woodford Reserve Double Double Oaked, matured in three barrels, and annual releases of the Master's Collection.

WOODFORD RESERVE DISTILLER'S SELECT
45.2% ABV (90.4 proof)
Aromas include rich, intense caramel and vanilla with dark cherries and oranges that carry into the palate along with cinnamon, nutmeg, and layers of roasted nuts. The long, smooth, balanced finish imparts caramel, vanilla, fruit, and spice.

WOODFORD RESERVE DOUBLE OAKED
45.2% ABV (90.4 proof)
Sweeter than Distiller's Select, it evokes caramel apple, maple syrup, macadamia nuts, and cinnamon sugar cookie. It features a silky mouthfeel with a light touch of honeyed oak in the finish. A very fine after-dinner sip.

MASTER DISTILLER ELIZABETH McCALL

Many modern master distillers came to their jobs with backgrounds in chemical engineering or an abiding love for whiskey. Not so Elizabeth McCall. "In 2009, at a graduation party for my little brother, I heard about an entry-level position as a sensory technician at Brown-Forman." Another party guest had overheard McCall talking about completing her master's degree in counseling and psychology and her frustration with finding a job. "He said, 'We have somebody leaving a position, and they typically hire people with psychology backgrounds for reading human response to product.' It was a good fit, too, because I could do the statistical analysis and knew the methodology of setting up experiments."

McCall, who drank the occasional beer or vodka tonic, soon appreciated the flavor complexity of Bourbon. She also learned to trace sources of off notes in the samples that came

to her lab. Soon, she was sharing her sensory expertise with Brown-Forman staff in Tennessee, Canada, Mexico, and Finland.

In February 2014, her trajectory changed again. "I took an internal educational class with Chris Morris. For a week, we went to different distilleries around Kentucky. We did food-and-spirits pairings, learning about all the spirits that we made and from some of our competitors. I asked him if I could help. I would get there early, and I wasn't trying to be a brownnoser. I was genuinely curious. Chris always says that that made an impact on him, and he was like, 'Who's this young woman?'"

Morris asked McCall whether she wanted to train as a master taster, which she did, and she started working on the Old Forester and Woodford Reserve brands. In 2016, she became the master taster for Woodford Reserve. "I enjoyed speaking with people, and I just loved talking about the flavor profiles. It seemed like a natural fit for me."

A few years later, she rose to assistant master distiller. "That was when it shifted to learning the innovation decisions that only a master distiller can make, like when there's a proof issue, a color issue, or we had an oops in the distillery—then turning that oops into something awesome. He taught me how he navigates all those things."

When she took that entry-level job in 2009, McCall had no intention of assuming one of the most visible positions in the American whiskey industry. Her career goal was much more modest: "I've always wanted to make enough money to support my habit of riding horses and to be able to go on vacation once a year."

Kentucky Artisan Distillery

Founded in 1997

KentuckyArtisanDistillery.com
6230 Old LaGrange Road
Crestwood, KY 40014

In 1995, Steve Thompson stepped down as president of Brown-Forman, deciding to open his own distillery rather than run someone else's. In Oldham County, about 20 miles northeast of Louisville, he and business partners Chris Miller and Mike Lor-

ing bought a former ice cream factory and opened Kentucky Artisan Distillery (KAD) in 1997.

KAD buys a large portion of its grain from the 700-acre Waldeck Farm, a mile up the road. They give the spent mash to farmers in Oldham and

Henry Counties for livestock feed. Most American distilleries buy their malt from suppliers, but KAD has its own malting room, where they wet the barley, sprout it, and dry it—the process that produces the enzymes that metabolize the mash starches into sugar that yeast turns into alcohol. Thompson collected antique distillery equipment, and KAD uses four different stills, one of which dates to just after Prohibition. They all have names: Jeffery, Ginger, and the Bean for the pot stills, and the column still is Mia. Shelves in the tasting room display pieces of equipment from Thompson's collection, which rotate on a regular basis.

KAD brands include Whiskey Row Bourbon and Billy Goat Strut American Whiskey, and the distillery also does contract-distilling for clients, most notably Jefferson's Bourbon. In 1997, Trey Zoeller started that brand when he and his father, Chet, bought barrels languishing in the warehouse of the

closed Stitzel-Weller Distillery (page 53). It seems hard to believe now, but in the 1980s and '90s, a glut of aging whiskey was sitting in Kentucky warehouses. Zoeller oversees some sourcing and all production of various Jefferson's expressions, including Jefferson's Ocean. After distillation and barreling, those barrels go onto a research ship that tracks sharks for scientific purposes and spends several months at sea, which may sound gimmicky, but the resulting whiskey does have a slightly briny flavor. Each release receives a voyage number.

KAD also distills Burks Spring, a brand first released in 2024 by Dick Burks, a descendent of the distiller whose Burks Spring Distillery Bill and Marge Samuels bought in 1953 to start Maker's Mark (page 61).

> If you visit KAD, check out Yew Dell Gardens next door, a 60-acre botanical garden and arboretum.

Recommended Bottles

VALUE
Whiskey Row Small Batch Bourbon Whiskey
Jefferson's Reserve

SPECIAL OCCASION
Burks Springs Bottled-in-Bond Bourbon
Jefferson's Ocean Aged at Sea

Tasting Notes

The portfolio of Jefferson's Bourbons continues growing with limited releases often finished in barrels that contained other spirits. Worth trying, they usually fall in the price ranges of special occasion or splurge. If investing in a bottle feels daunting, look for them at a good Bourbon bar (page 205).

WHISKEY ROW
SMALL BATCH BOURBON

mash bill not released, no age statement, 44% ABV (88 proof)

It has aromas of caramel corn with some lemon peel and new leather and flavors of rich vanilla with persistent citrus, some cinnamon sugar, and a little cocoa powder. The medium-long finish ends with a little oak.

JEFFERSON'S RESERVE

mash bill not released, "Very Old" (probably double-digit aging), 45.1% ABV (90.2 proof)

Toffee and a fruit salad of apples, plums, and berries dominate both the nose and palate. Savory notes of leather and tobacco provide counterpoint before everything gradually fades to some sweet oak and light pepper.

BURKS SPRINGS
BOTTLED-IN-BOND BOURBON

60% corn, 25% rye, 15% malted barley; 5 years old; 50% ABV (100 proof)

Some cinnamon and rich notes of vanilla pudding balance dark brown sugar with mixed berries and cherries. In a second sip, the fruit becomes figs, which eventually yield to a finish of oak and white pepper.

Michter's Distillery

Founded in 2000

Michters.com
801 West Main Street
Louisville, KY 40202

The modern Michter's started in 2000, but it can lay claim to the oldest lineage of any of today's American distilleries. In 1753, John Shenk and his brother Michael, both Swiss-Mennonite farmers and distillers, opened a distillery on Snitzel Creek in Lebanon County, Pennsylvania. The brothers made rye whiskey, using the grain that grew best in the area. Lore holds that General George Washington purchased their whiskey to fortify his troops during the Continental Army's winter encampment at Valley Forge from 1777 to 1778.

In the 1780s, the Shenks enlarged their distillery, and Michael's son-in-law Rudolph Meyer managed it, producing much of the rye whiskey consumed in nearby Philadelphia. In 1827, Elizabeth Shenk Kratzer, John's great-granddaughter, inherited the operation, and her husband, John, ran it until she sold it to Abe Bomberger, a relative. Bomberger and his sons operated it until Prohibition forced it to close in 1920.

After Prohibition, the Bomberger Distillery reopened and passed through a series of owners until the 1950s, when Lou Forman purchased it, renaming it Michter's, a portmanteau of "Michael" and "Peter," his sons' names (pronounced MICK-turz, not MITCH-turz). The downturn in demand for American whiskey forced Michter's to close in 1989, and the company sold the copper pot stills to a craft distiller in the aptly named Chagrin, Ohio.

Although gone, the Michter's brand still retained a devoted following. In the 1990s, one of those followers, Joe Magliocco, bought the rights to the name, along with industry consultant Richard Newman, and they revived the brand, this time producing Bourbon and rye. The same downturn that had precipitated the closure of the Pennsylvania distillery resulted in a surfeit of unsold barrels aging in Kentucky warehouses. Magliocco moved Michter's to Kentucky, the historic home of Bourbon production, and bought some of that dormant stock to release under the Michter's name. A supply of these older, sourced whiskeys still sees very limited releases. Magliocco also hired highly experienced distillers to oversee barrel aging and to start distilling Michter's own juice.

Willy Pratt, who had worked at Brown-Forman for decades, led the first distilling, using the facilities at other distilleries. Pam Heilmann, who had worked at Beam's Booker Noe Distillery, succeeded him. After

▲ Joe Magliocco, CEO of Michter's

▲ Dan McKee, master distiller of Michter's

she retired came current master distiller Dan McKee, who had worked as distillery manager under Heilmann. In 2012, Michter's dedicated distillery opened in Shively. Not open to the public, it produces the latest in a line of expressions regarded highly by the industry and consumers. Over the years, the sourced, contract-distilled, and original-production whiskeys have garnered many top ratings and awards.

In 2012, Michter's also helped start the revitalization of Louisville's West Main Street as the first brand to commit to locating a visitor attraction on Whiskey Row. The company purchased the 19th-century Fort Nelson building, a former warehouse made of brick, stone, and cast iron and topped with a distinctive turret—that, it turned out, proved structurally unsound. It took seven years and about $8 million to make the building and its 27-foot-wide interior safe. It was worth the wait.

From the original Michter's, three cedar fermentation tanks nestle against one wall. Opposite stands the pair of copper pot stills made by Vendome in 1976 that had gone from Pennsylvania to Ohio. Distillery supervisor Jordan Hamilton presides over the 550-gallon beer still and 110-gallon doubler, which Magliocco acquired when production outgrew the still's capacity. At the back of the building, the tasting room features racks of barrels and large windows overlooking the Ohio River. In 2017, Michter's bought a 205-acre farm in Springfield, Kentucky, which grows non-GMO corn, rye, and barley used in both distillery locations.

At the Fort Nelson location, you can choose from several different tours, and all include tastings of multiple Michter's whiskeys. The high-end tour includes the opportunity to fill, seal, and label a personalized, cask-strength whiskey straight from the barrel. But you don't need to book a tour to visit The Bar on the second floor and enjoy the cocktail list created by cocktail expert and historian David Wondrich, PhD, the James Beard Award–winning author of *Imbibe!*, which helped revive the work of Jerry Thomas, author of the world's first cocktail guide. Flights in The Bar may include older and limited-edition whiskeys. The Bar doesn't have a food menu, but each table receives a small tray of crunchy nibbles.

A landing outside the bar offers a fine viewpoint into the distillery. Inside, tables offer picturesque views of the stone and cast-iron facades of other historic buildings on Main Street. Look west for a glimpse of the seven-story Louisville Slugger leaning against the bat factory and museum.

Recommended Bottles

Michter's standard portfolio contains several whiskeys that retail for less than $50 but none under $40. The limited editions, some of them annual releases, retail for more than $100. The double-digit aged whiskeys retail for much more. To sample a variety, visit a well-stocked whiskey bar or the Fort Nelson Distillery. The Sour Mashes and American Whiskeys qualify neither as Bourbon nor rye because they don't contain at least 51 percent corn or rye, or because they age in barrels already used for aging whiskey.

VALUE

Michter's US★1 Straight Bourbon

Michter's US★1 Unblended Small Batch American Whiskey

Michter's US★1 Straight Rye Whiskey

Michter's American Whiskey

Michter's US★1 Sour Mash Whiskey

SPLURGE

Michter's Toasted Barrel Bourbon

Michter's 10 Year Old Bourbon

Michter's Barrel Finish Bourbon

Bomberger's Declaration Bourbon

Michter's Toasted Barrel Finish Rye

Shenk's Homestead Sour Mash

Tasting Notes

Michter's doesn't release its mash bills.

MICHTER'S US★1 STRAIGHT BOURBON

45.7% ABV (91.4 proof)

Balanced and layered, it imparts caramel, sour cherries, and cinnamon sugar, with some new saddle leather and a little sweet pipe tobacco. Add a few drops of water for more baking spices and even a little bit of root beer.

MICHTER'S 10 YEAR OLD BOURBON

47.2% ABV (94.4 proof)

It suggests caramel-covered toffee candy bar studded with raisins, dried cherries, and hazelnuts. It drinks very smooth, with lots of honeycomb on the finish. Perfect to savor after dinner.

MICHTER'S BARREL STRENGTH BOURBON

54.2% ABV (108.4 proof) (varies by release)

The consummate Kentucky Hug, it offers aromas of crème brûlée, ripe apples, and a touch of cinnamon sugar. The same flavors alternate between melding together and pinging individually with a little savory spice and a long, warm finish.

BOMBERGER'S DECLARATION BOURBON

54% ABV (108 proof)

On the nose, milk chocolate warms to apple peel, and it offers a medley of baking spices on the palate, like apple cobbler drizzled with caramel. Add a little water for a fruit explosion.

ANDREA WILSON, COO AND MASTER OF MATURATION

A chemical engineer by training, Andrea Wilson possesses a wealth of experience. For many years, she worked for Diageo, rising to direct distillation and maturation in North America and helping guide the growth of Bulleit Bourbon (page 71). She served as the first woman chair of the board of the Kentucky Distillers' Association, and the Kentucky Bourbon Hall of Fame inducted her in 2022. At Michter's, she describes her role as being "responsible for everything after distillation." She and her warehouse team of about a dozen people oversee barrel-entry proof, wood seasoning, and specifications for toasting and charring.

By law, distillate can't go into barrels at any more than 62.5 percent ABV (125 proof). A few distilleries use lower entry proofs, reasoning that extra water in the barrels acts as a solvent for flavorful compounds extracted from the wood during aging. Michter's has a barrel-entry proof of 103 (51.5 percent ABV), among the lowest in the industry.

For barrel staves, most Bourbon distilleries air-dry and season wood for six months. Michter's seasons its wood for 18 months "and sometimes up to five years," says Wilson. "The wood is sitting outside, which is different from kiln drying. When it's sitting outside, you're changing the wood chemically and microbiologically because it's being exposed to the elements, fungi, and lichens. They metabolize compounds and give way to other beautiful aromatics and characters that you want in your spirits."

Before assembly into barrels, the wood undergoes an application of heat, either slow toasting, in which the heat source doesn't touch the wood, or charring, in which a flame burns the wood directly. "Toasting is an art," says Wilson. "It's been around for a long time, and many winemakers use it to take advantage of the many natural extractives that exist within the wood itself. You can have hundreds of different profiles with toasting."

Charring matters "because it's an adsorption layer," she says, meaning that it allows the whiskey to move into the wood. "It's powerful as an accent to flavor. Lower chars can help accentuate fruit esters or spice characters, whereas darker chars will help accentuate darker char-

acteristics like chocolates or espressos, as well as accentuate smokiness."

After the spirit enters the barrel, Wilson supervises aging, which includes monitoring warehouse temperatures. "Kentucky is a great location because we have all these beautiful seasonal changes which create different temperatures and conditions for the whiskey to warm or cool inside the barrel based just on the natural environment, the atmosphere around us. When whiskey is getting warm, it's very volatile. It wants to expand into the capillaries of the wood. That's what creates the interaction with all the beautiful wood extractives as well as the other chemistry. When the whiskey cools, it pulls out of the wood and moves back to the center of the barrel."

Michter's has heated warehouses, one of only a handful of Kentucky distilleries. "In winter, the cask isn't as active," notes Wilson, which is when Michter's turns on the heat. "The idea is to increase the maturing quality of the spirit by increasing the interaction between the wood and the spirit. It's a very artistic process because, once you receive the distillate from the distilling side of the business, how do you want to influence that spirit? Do you want it to pull some vanilla out of the wood? Some caramel? Do you want it to lift the fruit? Do you want some spice? Some smokiness? Some chocolate? There are so many specifications with the wood that can influence the final product. There's a lot of art and a lot of science, but it's also about details, which can have a profound effect on the final product. That's what makes Kentucky Bourbon so great because we're not all doing it the same way. Those little details matter."

RockCastle
Bourbon

1/13/22
110.5prf
15351

Barrel House Distilling Co.

Lexington, KY

DSP-KY-15005

Barrel House Distilling Company

Founded in 2008

BarrelHouseDistillery.com
1200 Manchester Street
Lexington, KY 40504

W hen Jeff Wiseman and Pete Wright installed their small distillery in the building where James E. Pepper (page 97) once poured new-make whiskey into barrels, they unknowingly sparked the revitalization of the Lexington Distillery District. While their Bourbon was maturing, they released rum, vodka, and "moonshine" (flavored new-make whiskey). Here, they use 200-gallon, industrial-grade plastic bins as fermentation "tanks," and the rest of the production process operates on a similarly small scale. Barrel-strength RockCastle ages in barrels smaller than the industry standard (53 gallons). Proofed with Appalachian spring water, their Select Bourbon comes from only three 53-gallon barrels, making it small-batch, indeed.

The tour showcases the history of the site, the pair of copper pot stills used for distillation, and, of course, a tasting. The Elkhorn tavern next door uses a variety of Barrel House spirits in its craft cocktails, including an Elkhorn Smash made with Select Bourbon and red wine.

With the success of the Bourbon category at large and the growth of the company itself, Barrel House is expanding. Scheduled to welcome visitors in 2025, a second distillery in Cynthiana, about 30 miles northeast of Lexington, will allow more production of Bourbon and other spirits. It also will feature an event space with a kitchen available for rental.

Recommended Bottles

VALUE
Barrel House Select Bourbon

SPLURGE
Barrel House Cask Strength
RockCastle Kentucky Straight Bourbon

Tasting Notes

BARREL HOUSE SELECT BOURBON

Mash bill not released ("high rye" according to the tour), no age statement ("about 3 years"), 45% ABV (90 proof)

You'll find vanilla and fresh honeysuckle aromas, with some honey, cardamom, and orange peel on the palate. The rich mouthfeel ends with a long, sweet-spicy finish.

ROCKCASTLE KENTUCKY STRAIGHT BOURBON

Mash bill not released ("high rye"), 2 years old, 56.3% ABV (112.5 proof) (varies by release)

Buttered popcorn and some vanilla caramel carry into light citrus and some peppery spice. Small barrel aging adds quite a bit of oakiness.

James E. Pepper Distilling Company

Founded in 2008

JamesEPepper.com
1228 Manchester Street
Lexington, KY 40504

Elijah Pepper, a farmer-distiller, moved to Kentucky in 1776 and by 1812 had opened a distillery on Glenns Creek that eventually became Woodford Reserve (page 75). James E. Pepper, his grandson, adopted the elder Pepper's slogan, "Born with the Republic," for his own whiskey when he founded James E. Pepper and Company on Town Branch Creek in Lexington in 1879. The distillery released the James E. Pepper and Old Henry Clay brands, the latter named for the Bourbon-loving statesman from Lexington who had served as Speaker of the House and a US senator.

The Old-Fashioned cocktail wasn't invented at Louisville's Pendennis Club in honor of Colonel Pepper, but he may have introduced the drink to the Waldorf Astoria hotel in New York City, where he stayed frequently.

In the 1890s, a series of economic depressions occurred, and Pepper found himself caught in one. In 1896, several of his creditors demanded payment, and such was Pepper's prominence that the *New York Times* reported on his financial woes. To meet his debts, he had to auction off his large stable of racehorses. But his wife, Ella O. Pepper, came to his rescue. At the auction, she used her own money to bid on the thoroughbreds. When the other bidders saw what she was doing, they respectfully halted their efforts. Ella saved both the racing stable and the distillery.

The distillery's museum relates that piece of Pepper history, among others. After Ella's bailout, whiskey production grew, and the company prospered, but in December 1906, James Pepper slipped on an icy sidewalk in New York City, hit his head, and lapsed into a coma from which he never recovered. The distillery subsequently passed through a series of owners,

LEXINGTON DISTILLERY DISTRICT

The Pepper Distillery anchors the 25-acre Distillery District, wedged between a network of railroad tracks and Town Branch Creek. Unlike Louisville's Whiskey Row, lined with elegant 19th-century facades, Lexington's district has a gritty, industrial feel perfectly appropriate to its history. Besides Pepper, the area has only one other distillery: Barrel House (page 95). Town Branch Distillery (page 129) lies only a mile away, but on the other side of a four-lane highway that defines part of the district's boundary. Other area businesses include live-music venues, cafés, an ice cream shop, casual restaurants, a brewery, gift shops, and a retro gaming arcade. For more information, visit LexingtonDistilleryDistrict.com.

including eventually Schenley Distillers Company. In the 1930s, they demolished the older frame buildings on the property to build brick-and-concrete warehouses for whiskey storage. Closed in 1967, the buildings sat abandoned for almost half a century.

In 2008, with profits from an Irish whiskey brand, Amir Peay bought and restored the Pepper buildings. The time-consuming project included sinking a well on-site for limestone-filtered water and installing a 27-foot-tall Vendome column still. Distilling began in the new facility in 2017. The modern Pepper releases include Bourbons, ryes, and an American single malt.

Recommended Bottles

Before production began and distiller Aaron Schorsch's creations had matured, Pepper sourced early releases, which still happens for blending what he produces in Lexington.

VALUE
James E. Pepper 1776 Straight Bourbon

SPECIAL OCCASION
Old Pepper Bottled-in-Bond Bourbon

SPLURGE
James E. Pepper Decanter Barrel Proof Bourbon

Tasting Notes

JAMES E. PEPPER 1776 STRAIGHT BOURBON
60% corn, 36% rye, 4% malted barley; no age statement but between 3 and 4 years old; 50% ABV (100 proof)
Quite a bit of rye leans into cloves, which vanilla, brown sugar, and some milk chocolate balance. Indulge the Pepper legend and make an Old-Fashioned with it.

MB Roland Distillery

Founded in 2009

MBRoland.com
137 Barkers Mill Road
Pembroke, KY 42266

Paul and Merry Beth (née Roland) Tomaszewski wanted to practice grain-to-glass distilling to connect to the heritage of farm distillers who lived in the 1700s and 1800s. They started their distillery on a former Amish dairy farm, and while small in scale compared to the legacy giants of central Kentucky, MB Roland has a large portfolio of spirits that includes Bourbon, rye, malt whiskey, and moonshines (flavored new-make whiskeys).

A white-frame farmhouse contains the tasting room and gift shop, the covered front porch serving as the stage for summer concerts. Across the lawn, the distillery building has a pair of modified pot stills. The whiskey ages in the former cow barn, which the Tomaszewskis have retrofitted with barrel ricks. What looks perhaps like an outhouse is a smokehouse—but not for bacon and hams. Paul smokes a good portion of the corn that goes into their whiskey, giving some of them a flavor profile best described as "Kentucky peated."

▲ The grain-to-glass distillery is located on a former Amish farm.

▲ Corn is smoked in the smokehouse to create their unique "Kentucky peated" flavor profile.

Tomaszewski also likes to mentor other aspiring distillers. A few years ago, a woman whose husband was stationed at nearby Fort Campbell army base took a distillery tour. Sydney Jones asked so many detailed, knowledgeable questions that Tomaszewski offered her a job. After learning her craft at MB Roland and another distillery in Florida, Jones served as head distiller at FEW Spirits in Evanston, Illinois. Currently, she is the supervisor and lead distillery technician at Heaven Hill's new distillery near Bardstown.

Recommended Bottles

SPECIAL OCCASION

MB Roland Kentucky Straight Bourbon Whiskey

MB Roland Kentucky Straight Wheat Bourbon

MB Roland Dark Fired Kentucky Straight Bourbon Whiskey

Barker's Mill Bottled-in-Bond Straight Bourbon Whiskey

Tasting Notes

Rather than yellow dent field corn, the most widely used for American whiskeys, MB Roland uses locally grown white sweet corn. The distillery doesn't filter any of its Bourbons, ryes, or malt whiskeys, bottling all at barrel strength. Tasting notes and proofs vary by batch and bottling.

MB ROLAND KENTUCKY STRAIGHT BOURBON WHISKEY

78% white corn, 17% rye, 5% malted barley; at least 2 years old; 53.5% ABV (107 proof)

It evokes corncrib on a warm summer's day with some apple peel and sweet oak. Some cinnamon and dark chocolate provide counterpoint.

MB ROLAND DARK FIRED KENTUCKY STRAIGHT BOURBON WHISKEY

45% white corn, 33% dark fired corn, 17% rye, 5% malted barley; 2 years old; 57.4% ABV (114.8 proof)

It suggests smoked corn on the cob with caramelized dark brown sugar and mixed berries. The fruit never surrenders to the smoke and carries through the finish.

BARKER'S MILL KENTUCKY STRAIGHT BOURBON WHISKEY BOTTLED-IN-BOND

white corn, red winter wheat, and malted barley (percentages not disclosed); at least 4 years old; 50% ABV (100 proof)

Sweet malt and honey characterize this impressively smooth sipper. Notes of apple and a whisper of cinnamon round out the flavor profile.

Louisville Distilling Company

Founded in 2010

AngelsEnvy.com
500 East Main Street
Louisville, KY 40202

In 2004, Lincoln Henderson—Brown-Forman's master distiller and a member of the Kentucky Bourbon Hall of Fame—retired from the beverage giant, where he had overseen Woodford Reserve (page 75). But he didn't want to stay out of Bourbon. In 2006, he broached the idea of starting a new distillery to his son Wes. He planned to use the same mash bill as Woodford Reserve and Brown-Forman's other Bourbon, Old Forester, but then take it a step beyond. He proposed finishing the aged Bourbon in ex-Port barrels.

"The Port finishing was both controversial and innovative at the time," says Owen Martin, current master distiller for Angel's Envy. "Scotch whisky had been aged in ex-Sherry barrels for years, but that kind of finishing was completely unknown in Bourbon." Controversy arose from the government standards stipulating that producers can add no flavoring or coloring to Bourbon. Detractors argued that secondary aging was adding Port to the whiskey. So Angel's Envy made it clear on the label, "Kentucky Straight Bourbon Whiskey Finished in Port Wine Barrels," which satisfied regulators.

The restored 19th-century building that houses the distillery formerly served as a Vermont American power tool factory. Lincoln Henderson's father worked there, and as a child, he visited his dad there. But Lincoln Henderson died before ground broke on the facility, which became the first full production distillery in downtown Louisville. The name riffs on the "angel's share" of whiskey that evaporates from barrels as it ages. Henderson wanted to make a Bourbon that the angels would be sorry they couldn't experience. Wes Henderson and his son Kyle brought Angel's Share to fruition and created a pair of signature products—the ex-Port Bourbon and an ex-rum rye sourced from MGP in Indiana and aged secondarily in Kentucky—before

Recommended Bottles

VALUE
Angel's Envy Kentucky Straight Bourbon
  Finished in Port Wine Barrels

SPECIAL OCCASION
Angel's Envy Cask Strength Bottled-in-Bond
Angel's Envy Straight Rye Whiskey Finished in
  Caribbean Rum Casks

SPLURGE
Angel's Envy Cask Strength Kentucky Straight
  Bourbon Finished in Port Wine Barrels (annual
  release)

Tasting Notes

**ANGEL'S ENVY KENTUCKY
STRAIGHT BOURBON FINISHED
IN PORT WINE BARRELS**
*72% corn, 18% rye, 10% malted barley;
no age statement; 43.3% ABV
(86.6 proof)*
It smells vanilla-forward with notes
of dried fruit, some sorghum, sugar-
coated almonds, and a bit of oak.
The Port finishing emerges as a pop
of wine fruit on the finish.

**ANGEL'S ENVY CASK STRENGTH
KENTUCKY STRAIGHT BOURBON
FINISHED IN PORT WINE BARRELS, 2023**
*72% corn, 18% rye, 10% malted barley; no age state-
ment; 59.1% ABV (118.2 proof)*
Waves of vanilla, cherries, cocoa, and cherry cola
on the nose carry to the palate, where marshmallow and rich caramel join them. The velvety
mouthfeel leads into a long finish with notes of
citrus and red wine

eventually selling the distillery to Bacardi. Today, any objections about the Port finishing have all but vanished, and Henderson's innovation has inspired scores of brands to use barrels that once held Cabernet Sauvignon, Pinot Noir, oloroso Sherry, Cognac, Armagnac, Curaçao, and beer.

Brightly lit by high windows, the distillery tour highlights the 43-foot-tall column still visible from Main Street, and many a visitor selfie has captured the spirit safe, shaped like the distinctive bottle, which sits on a glass plinth etched with a pair of angel's wings. An elegant bar on the second floor serves craft cocktails and hosts events. A tasting room branches off to one side..

MASTER DISTILLER OWEN MARTIN

Angel's Envy has a short history compared to legacy distilleries, and master distiller Owen Martin, who joined the fold in 2022, knows that what he does both honors and builds on Lincoln Henderson's idea of finishing whiskey in barrels that once held other spirits. "As a company that has only ever made finished whiskeys, why not make an unfinished whiskey, but make it bottled-in-bond, something that has a historical significance?" says Martin. "Let's combine two categories: bottled-in-bond and cask strength."

The barrels from which the new expression comes were laid down in 2018 and palletized rather than laid on their sides. The barrel-entry proof ran low at 103 (51.5 percent ABV), and the whiskey lost proof over the years, dropping to 99 proof (49.5 percent ABV). By adding a tiny amount of slightly higher proof Bourbon, Martin attained the 50 percent ABV (100 proof) needed for bottled-in-bond. But it still counts as cask strength because it came straight from the barrel, untouched by water, at 50 percent ABV. You can buy Angel's Envy unfinished Bourbon only in the distillery's gift shop.

Limestone Branch Distillery

Founded in 2010

LimestoneBranch.com
1280 Veterans Memorial Parkway
Lebanon, KY 40033

Growing up, brothers Stephen and Paul Beam knew how deep their Kentucky distilling roots ran. Their surname rings with history in the Bourbon industry, and their mother descends from Joseph Washington Dant, who started making whiskey in Kentucky in 1836. The Dant family distilled until Prohibition and again afterward, but the Bourbon downturn of the 1970s put them out of business once more.

Displays at the Limestone Branch Distillery, which the brothers launched in 2010, showcase both sides of their family with memorabilia including whiskey jugs, bottles, bar trays, photos, and ads for various family brands. They revived Yellowstone, a textbook example of how a brand can take a winding journey through multiple owners. The Bluegrass State has its own national park, Mammoth Cave, so why name the whiskey for another one that stretches across Wyoming, Montana, and Idaho? In 1872, their ancestor J. Bernard Dant launched the brand to commemorate the opening of Yellowstone as America's first national park. The original label depicted the Upper Falls of the Yellowstone River. Later, when Glenmore owned the brand, the image on the label changed to Old Faithful, the iconic geyser. Glenmore sold the brand to Heaven Hill, which almost immediately sold it to David Sherman Company, a distributor in St. Louis that later renamed itself LuxCo. In 2015, Stephen Beam formed a partnership with LuxCo to use his forebear's brand name. Limestone Branch makes the Bourbon, LuxCo distributes it, and the label has reverted to the original waterfall.

> If you visit, make time for a tour of the Kentucky cooperage of Independent Stave Company, the world's largest maker of barrels for aging spirits, also in Lebanon. For more information, visit KentuckyCooperageTours.com.

▲ Joseph Washington Dant

In addition to the Beam and Dant exhibits, notable features of the Limestone Branch tour include a pot still made by Hoga, a Portuguese company, and Minor's Lounge, a tasting room and cocktail bar named for Minor Case Beam, another of the brothers' forebears. They named their excellent Minor Case rye whiskey for him, too. Limestone Branch also makes Yellowstone American Single Malt Whiskey and Bowling & Burch Gin.

Recommended Bottles

VALUE

Yellowstone Select Kentucky Straight Bourbon
  Whiskey

SPECIAL OCCASION

Private barrel select, barrel proof Bourbons, any

Tasting Notes

YELLOWSTONE SELECT KENTUCKY STRAIGHT BOURBON WHISKEY

Mash bill not released, no age statement (between 5 and 7 years, according to the distillery), 46.5% ABV (93 proof)

Aromas include vanilla, oak, and cherry circling one another, with some brown sugar, leather, and ripe peach balancing them. Overall, it tastes very smooth. It tends toward sweetness but never cloying, thanks to the oak and a note of multigrain cereal.

Bluegrass Distillers

Founded in 2012

BluegrassDistillers.com

DOWNTOWN
501 West 6th Street #165
Lexington, KY 40508

ELKWOOD FARM
158 West Leestown Road
Midway, KY, 40347

Sam Rock and Nathan Brown, friends and business partners, started their distillery with a small budget. Rock learned how to make Bourbon by watching YouTube videos. For their first fermenters, they used 5-gallon buckets that they stirred with a boat oar. Eventually, they scaled up and found a space in the Bread Box building, built around 1900, in Lexington's Northside neighborhood. It contains their 250-gallon Portuguese pot still, barrel storage, and retail shop.

As of 2024, Bluegrass Distillers can produce about one 53-gallon barrel of Bourbon per day, but production will increase dramatically in 2025 or 2026 when its new distillery opens in Midway. The 62-acre Elkwood Farm campus includes a handsome red-brick house dating from the mid-1830s. The house serves as the visitor center, tasting room, and retail shop. The new distillery will have a 40-foot copper column capable of producing more than 1 million gallons of distillate annually.

> The Bread Box building takes its name from the Rainbo Bread factory, which it housed for decades. Today it contains other businesses, including a brewery and seafood restaurant.

Recommended Bottles

SPECIAL OCCASION
Bluegrass Distillers Blue Corn Bourbon Bottled-in-Bond
Bluegrass Distillers High Rye Bourbon
Bluegrass Distillers Toasted Oak
Bluegrass Distillers Kentucky Straight Bourbon Whiskey Wheated Bottled-in-Bond

Tasting Notes

BLUEGRASS DISTILLERS BLUE CORN BOURBON BOTTLED-IN-BOND
75% blue corn, 21% wheat, 4% malted barley; 4 years old; 50% ABV (100 proof)
It smells pleasantly yeasty with the aroma of rising multigrain bread and a whiff of malt. It tastes primarily of butterscotch with stone fruit, apples, and a pinch of baking spice arriving at the finish.

Old Pogue Distillery

Founded in 2012

OldPogue.com
715 Germantown Road
Maysville, KY 41056

The town of Maysville, called Limestone until incorporated in 1787, holds special significance in Bourbon history. In the early 1800s, it served as a major port for shipping whiskey down the Ohio and Mississippi Rivers as far as New Orleans. In 1821, Stout & Adams of Maysville offered "Bourbon whiskey" for sale, the first known use of "Bourbon" to signify the whiskey. Henry E. Pogue and John H. Thomas founded the H. E. Pogue Distillery here in 1870. Old Time, their flagship Bourbon, did well, and by 1900, Pogue's warehouses contained about 27,000 barrels. Like so many others, the distillery closed with Prohibition, but the whiskey on hand had a new, illegal future.

In 1920, George Remus of Cincinnati purchased a part interest in the distillery. Two months later, he bought a small pharmacy in Covington, Kentucky, across the Ohio River from Cincinnati, which he renamed the Kentucky Drug Company. Armed with several medicinal whiskey licenses, most of them forgeries, Remus sold whiskey, including Pogue's, on the black market. At one time, Remus controlled about a third of all bootleg spirits sales in America. When the Pogues realized what was happening with their Bourbon, they pressed Remus for proper paperwork. Repeated lawsuits had no effect. After Repeal, the distillery resumed production before passing into the hands of Schenley Distillers, which closed it for

good in the 1950s. Fire destroyed the abandoned distillery in 1973.

Despite the venture's rocky history, the Pogue family went back into the whiskey business, though on a smaller scale. Next to the historic Pogue family home—a beautiful, three-story, white brick house on a steep bluff overlooking the Ohio River—they built a microdistillery in 2012. John Pogue, a geologist before becoming the family's distiller, makes the whiskey and conducts limited tours of the distilling operation and the house. The house contains displays of family artifacts and memorabilia and, from the balcony, offers sweeping views of the river and town below, a highlight of the tour. You have to book distillery tours online, and availability can prove limited. In 2018, the company opened the Old Pogue Experience in downtown Maysville to allow more visitors to learn about the distillery. In addition to tastings and a retail shop, the newer location features a museum of American whiskey history with a focus on the Pogue Distillery.

Recommended Bottles

In addition to the regularly available small-batch Bourbon, John Pogue also releases Old Maysville Club, a bottled-in-bond Kentucky straight rye malt whiskey that uses a brand name from the original distillery.

SPECIAL OCCASION

Old Pogue Master's Select Small Batch Bourbon
Old Maysville Club

Tasting Notes

OLD POGUE MASTER'S SELECT SMALL BATCH BOURBON

Mash bill not released, 9 years old, 45.5% ABV (91 proof)
It offers vanilla with some cherry and a lot of cinnamon. All the flavor notes take time to evolve through the pleasant viscosity. Just the right amount of oak prevents it from tasting too sweet.

Rabbit Hole Distillery

Founded in 2012

RabbitHoleDistillery.com
711 East Jefferson Street
Louisville, KY 40202

In the 1980s, most bars carried Beam Bourbons, Maker's Mark, or Jack Daniels Tennessee Whiskey. Chicago psychologist Kaveh Zamanian favored Scotch until he met his wife, Heather, a fourth-generation Kentuckian, who taught him the virtues of Bourbon. Not every Bourbon convert decides to open a distillery, but as Zamanian puts it, he fell down the rabbit hole. "When I was coming down here with Heather, I started tasting some dusties, such as Old Fitz[gerald] from 1962 or 63, and my question was: How come we're not getting these products on the shelf? I started looking at the history in terms of what happened pre-Prohibition, post-Prohibition, World War II to where we are now. There's something really beautiful about what goes into becoming a Bourbon. The idea of '51 percent corn, 49 percent possibility' popped into mind as a philosophy for Bourbon, and I thought, *There's an opportunity here to do something unique.*"

MARY DOWLING

By the mid-1880s, John and Mary Dowling owned three distilleries in Anderson County, Kentucky, including Waterfill & Frazier. With John's distilling skill and Mary's business acumen, they became wealthy. Dowling Hall, their Italianate mansion featuring a three-story tower at its front, still stands in Lawrenceburg. In 1908, John died suddenly, leaving the distillery to his wife, who ran it successfully until Prohibition.

Mary Dowling skirted Prohibition in one of the most unique ways known to history. She had the entire distillery disassembled, loaded on railroad cars, and transported to Juárez, Mexico. She hired Joe Beam as her distiller—who, after Repeal, helped the Shapiras launch Heaven Hill (page 45)—and made Bourbon there until 1964 when Congress passed the law stipulating that Bourbon could be made only in America (page xiv).

In 2023, Rabbit Hole released two Bourbons named for Mary Dowling and her Mexican venture. The 93-proof (46.5 percent ABV) expression finishes in ex-Tequila barrels, and the 107 proof (53.5 percent ABV) uses wheat in its mash bill.

That idea stayed with Zamanian until he finally took the plunge down his rabbit hole. In 2008, he and his family moved to Louisville, and he spent time talking with industry professionals, including Jim Rutledge of Four Roses; Dave Scheurich, who had been with Woodford Reserve; and barrel broker Richard Wolf. Rather than sourcing and blending whiskeys, as many startups do, Zamanian had his Bourbon and rye contract-distilled at New Riff (page 159). The Rabbit Hole Distillery—a gleaming, state-of-the-art facility of glass, copper, and steel—opened in Louisville's Nulu district in 2018. The whiskey on shelves now comes from that facility.

The design of the distillery deliberately realized Zamanian's desire to play with the possibility of the 49 percent of the mash bill not from corn. It can produce 27,000 barrels per year and run small, limited-release, and experimental whiskeys in batches of just 22 or 23 barrels. Many of those experiments finish in barrels other than oak or in barrels that held wine or other spirits.

The distillery and the tour offer striking transparency. The walls of the cooker and fermenter rooms consist of glass. Visible through glass panels on the floor, labeled pipes carry liquid from one piece of equipment to another. A third-floor bar features a pair of dedicated tasting rooms and expansive views of the surrounding cityscape.

Original artworks enliven the walls, and artist-commissioned labels—most depicting characters

from *Alice's Adventures in Wonderland* or Shakespeare's plays—adorn special Bourbons and ryes in the gift shop. "It's part of keeping that whimsical approach, that we have a little fun, but at the same time give our consumers something unique."

Recommended Bottles

SPECIAL OCCASION
Rabbit Hole Cavehill Kentucky Straight Bourbon
Rabbit Hole Heigold Kentucky Straight Bourbon
Rabbit Hole Dareringer Kentucky Straight
  Bourbon Whiskey
Distillery Series, any (released quarterly only at
  the gift shop)
Rabbit Hole Boxergrail Kentucky Straight Rye
  Whiskey

SPLURGE
Founder's Collection, any

Tasting Notes

RABBIT HOLE CAVEHILL KENTUCKY STRAIGHT BOURBON

70% corn, 10% malted wheat, 10% malted barley, 10% honey malt; 3 years old; 47.5% ABV (95 proof)
Aromas include chocolate-covered cherries and malted milk balls with honey and baking spices. Building on that foundation, the rich flavors add some orange zest, toffee, and cinnamon before transforming into some crème brûlée and drying to a finish featuring light pepper and oak.

RABBIT HOLE HEIGOLD KENTUCKY STRAIGHT BOURBON

70% corn, 25% rye, 5% malted barley; 3 years old; 47.5% ABV (95 proof)
Expect rich caramel, some molasses, and freshly grated ginger on the nose with a whiff of dried fruit. The savory palate evokes some herbal rye spice, butterscotch, and a hint of dried citrus. It drinks very smooth with oak, vanilla, and ginger on the finish.

RABBIT HOLE DARERINGER KENTUCKY STRAIGHT BOURBON WHISKEY

65% corn, 25% wheat, 10% malted barley, finished in ex–Pedro Ximénez Sherry casks; no age statement; 46.5% ABV (93 proof)
The nose features a basket of fruit: dark cherries, red raspberries, and Seville oranges, with some brown sugar. It tastes very fruity but balanced with rich caramel, marzipan, and some oak. The Sherry note resonates in the finish with some raisins and oak.

Town Branch Distillery

Founded in 2012

TownBranchBourbon.com
401 Cross Street
Lexington, KY 40508

A native Dubliner, Pearse Lyons had worked at the Guinness Brewery and earned his doctorate in yeast fermentation. He came to America and in 1980 started the Alltech company, which makes nutritional supplements for livestock, including racehorses. Hence he chose Lexington, the self-styled horse capital of the world, for founding his distillery.

Lyons missed the spirits business, so in 2000 he revived the old Lexington Brewing Company, aging ales in ex-Bourbon barrels, which gave them distinctly sweet flavor notes. A dozen years later, he built Town Branch Distillery, a handsome glass-and-stone facility complete with a pair of pot stills made by Forsyths, which became the first working distillery in Lexington since Prohibition. Together, the brewery

and distillery form Lexington Brewing & Distilling Company, one of only a handful of joint breweries and distilleries in the world. If you look closely, you'll see brass doorknockers at the entrance shaped like lions' heads, a charming play on the founder's name.

In 2018, parent company Alltech opened Dueling Barrels Brewery and Distillery in Pikeville, Kentucky, bringing economic development to the Appalachian community. The name plays on the two types of spirits made there and Pikeville as one of the settings for the infamous Hatfield and McCoy feud.

Recommended Bottles

Town Branch also makes rye and malt whiskey worth tasting.

VALUE
Town Branch Bourbon
Town Branch True Cask Bourbon Whiskey

Tasting Notes

The Town Branch mash bill reflects the founder's taste, with a high ratio of malted barley—72 percent corn, 13 percent rye, 15 percent malted barley—giving these Bourbons a notably different flavor profile from traditional Kentucky Bourbons.

TOWN BRANCH BOURBON

no age statement, 45% ABV (90 proof)
Sweet on the nose, it imparts aromas of vanilla, a whiff of berries, and brown sugar, but it tastes much drier on the palate. The barley gives it more of an Irish whiskey character but without the floral notes.

TOWN BRANCH TRUE CASK BOURBON WHISKEY

54.1% ABV (108.1 proof) (varies by batch)
The proof lends heft, but this smooth sipper exhibits lots of concentrated vanilla, sorghum, and lemon zest, with some saddle leather and oak.

Kentucky Peerless Distilling Company

Founded in 2013

KentuckyPeerless.com
120 North 10th Street
Louisville, KY 40202

Born in 1859, in what had been and later became Poland, Henry Kraver immigrated with his family to New York City, where, at age seven, he started selling newspapers on Manhattan street corners. At 19, he wanted to see more of America, so he boarded a riverboat and traveled downstream until he ran out of money at Henderson, Kentucky, about 125 miles southeast of Louisville. "I always wondered why he didn't stop in Louisville," muses Corky Taylor, his grandson. "It was a much bigger city, which would have seemed to have more opportunities for him."

In Henderson, Kraver swept floors at Puckett's, a bar and restaurant. Two years later, he owned the bar. His ambitions ran beyond saloon keeping, however. After five years of training at a bank in St. Louis, he returned to Henderson, where he still owned Puckett's and founded the First National Bank of Henderson. He was 32 years old and remained president of the bank until his death.

In 1881, Elijah W. Worsham and Joe B. Johnson, founded the E. W. Worsham Distillery, a modest facility tucked between the Louisville and Nashville Railroad line, Canoe Creek, and the not-coincidentally named Kraver Street. Worsham's sons, Anthony and Dewitt, also joined the Henderson business, which, in 1889, Kraver bought, renaming it Peerless after the flagship brand made there.

When Kraver bought the facility, it was producing just eight barrels a day—but he had plans. In 1894, Henderson passed an ordinance banning the sale of alcohol on Sundays. In Indiana, Kraver rented a house, in which he opened a new bar and hired a boat to ferry thirsty customers across the river at no charge. By 1900, production at the distillery had expanded to 200 barrels a day. At peak production, Peerless had 50,000 barrels aging in multiple warehouses, and its Bourbon sold in Chicago, St. Louis, and other major markets.

When Kraver saw Prohibition coming, he closed the distillery and sold the existing stock of 40,000 barrels to drugstore owner Charles Walgreen of Chicago, who made a fortune selling Peerless stock as medicinal whiskey throughout those 13 "dry" years. Kraver bought Chicago's famed Palmer House Hotel, which became his last major business deal because, on a visit to it, he fell down the grand staircase and suffered injuries that led to his death in 1938.

Kentucky Peerless Distillery tours recount these spirited pieces of history, and lucky visitors can hear some of them from Corky Taylor himself. After a successful career in finance, Taylor retired to Florida but "got bored walking on the beach every day." He knew about his grandfather's distillery and decided to resurrect the brand. He and son Carson, a building contractor, bought a former tobacco warehouse con-

structed at the end of the 1800s. The younger Taylor remodeled it into a distillery that, on Tenth Street, a block north of Main, serves as the westernmost attraction on Louisville's Whiskey Row (page 199).

The father-son team hired Caleb Kilburn, a young distiller inspired to pursue a career in whiskey after visiting the Buffalo Trace Distillery (page 3) as a teenager. The Taylors and Kilburn kept production small and used the sweet-mash process (page 141). Peerless first released a two-year-old rye, which retailed for more than $100, a seemingly risky gambit. But its debut garnered rave reviews in whiskey publications and won spirits competitions, earning Peerless a reputation for excellence. In 2023, Kilburn departed to start his own distillery in eastern Kentucky, East-

ern Light Distillery, which is scheduled to open in late 2025.

After maturing, Bourbon followed the rye, which today it outsells. Peerless sets barrel-entry proof for all its whiskeys at 107, low for the industry. Producing the whiskey that way costs more but can yield more intense and complex flavors. In addition to the flagship Peerless Small Batch Bourbon and Peerless Kentucky Straight Rye, the distillery regularly releases limited-edition whiskeys, everything bottled at barrel-strength and non-chill filtered.

VENDOME COPPER & BRASS WORKS

Tucked away on a side street of Louisville's Butchertown neighborhood stands one of the city's oldest family-owned and-operated businesses. Vendome Copper & Brass Works shines as the premier maker of distilling equipment in America and one of the largest in the world. It set the gold standard, so to speak, for copper, brass, and stainless-steel manufacturing equipment. Vendome makes custom pieces for distilleries, breweries, pharmaceutical companies, and even candymakers.

In the early 1900s, founder Elmore Sherman started his still business, which thrived until Prohibition. He remained in business during the dry years, thanks to a major contract. Henry Kraver sold his distillery equipment to a distillery in Vancouver, Canada, in 1917, hiring Sherman to dismantle it all, transport it to Canada, and reassemble it. The project took almost a year and a half, during which time Kraver provided housing for the Sherman family and schooling for the children.

Corky Taylor approached Rob Sherman—a member of the fourth generation of the Sherman family to run Vendome—to provide equipment for the revived company. In the process, Taylor discovered the historical connection between the two families, and Sherman credited Taylor's grandfather with ensuring the survival of Vendome Copper & Brass Works. For more information, visit VendomeCopper.com.

Recommended Bottles

SPECIAL OCCASION
Peerless Small Batch Bourbon
Peerless Small Batch Rye

SPLURGE
Peerless Toasted Bourbon
Peerless Small Batch Double Oak Bourbon
limited-release Bourbons or ryes, any

Tasting Notes

PEERLESS SMALL BATCH BOURBON
mash bill not released, 4 years old, 54.4% ABV (108.9 proof)
Layered, complex, and elegant, it imparts rich vanilla with pears, dark brown sugar, cinnamon, nutmeg, mace, and allspice. A little water reveals milk chocolate leading into a finish rich with oak and figs.

PEERLESS TOASTED BOURBON
mash bill not released, no age statement, 55% ABV (110 proof)
A complex mix of caramel, toffee, and dark brown sugar provides the backbone supporting multiple layers of crème brûlée, baking spices, honey, and cocoa. Apples and pears emerge with a little water.

Wilderness Trail

Founded in 2013

WildernessTrailDistillery.com
4095 Lebanon Road
Danville, KY 40422

Shane Baker and Pat Heist met in college and forged their friendship playing in a heavy-metal band. After college, the duo—now a mechanical engineer and microbiologist—started a business to meet the needs of the brewing and distilling industries in Kentucky and beyond. Ferm Solutions has become an international supplier of yeast and enzymes for fermentation and offers consulting services for troubleshooting beer or spirits with flavor flaws.

Work with and proximity to Kentucky distilleries inspired the pair to try distilling themselves. The first

Wilderness Trail "distillery" arose in a Ferm Solutions supply room outfitted with a 3-gallon pot still. It first released vodkas while its whiskey was aging.

Wilderness Trail didn't take long to outgrow that supply room. In 2016, Baker and Heist opened a discrete facility in Danville with six 20,000-gallon fermenters and two column stills, one 40 feet tall and another 43 feet tall. Why so much capacity? About 40 percent of their production goes to contract-distilling for clients. The tour showcases both stills and a view of the research-and-development lab occupied by white-coated staff. A

▲ Founders of Ferm Solutions and Wilderness Trail Distillery, Shane Baker (left) and Pat Heist (right) have been friends since college.

sign in the hallway window reads: "Observe Scientists in Their Natural Habitat." Ferm Solutions and the distillery continue to complement each other, with the lab maintaining quality control in the distillery and the distillery providing data for the lab.

In that lab, Heist oversees a living library of more than 50,000 strains of yeast and bacteria that helps identify which microbes cause which flavors. The bacteria come from fermentation vats at various client breweries and distilleries. During fermentation, different strains of yeast produce different esters, the aromatic compounds that generate the fruity or floral aromas and flavors in whiskey. Distillers must choose a yeast strain and mash bill very carefully, so startups from around the globe consult with Ferm Solutions to find the right combination for what they want to create.

On weekends, music lovers can hear Pat Heist as the lead singer in his rock band Zella May!

For its own products, Wilderness Trail uses the sweet-mash process instead of the more common sour mash, one of just a handful of distilleries to do so. The distillery produces two Bourbons—one with rye as its secondary grain and the other with wheat—and a rye, often releasing all three in cask-strength expressions as well. Their small batches come from no more than 12 barrels, and at 100 proof the distillery uses the lowest barrel-entry proof in the industry. That superlative proof allows more fermentation flavors to emerge in the finished whiskey.

THE SWEET-MASH PROCESS

Most distilleries use the sour-mash process, in which some liquid from the previous fermentation goes into a new fermentation to ensure consistent flavor and to lower the pH, making it more acidic and preventing bacterial contamination. The sweet-mash process uses no leftover mash, also called backset, from a previous fermentation. It requires more labor, including cleaning all the equipment between each batch. "I can reduce my potential for contamination just by keeping a very clean facility," explains Pat Heist. "When we designed our distillery, we made sure that everything was easy to clean. We don't have external heat exchangers. A lot of old distilleries have old-style, external heat exchangers that cool the mash to match the fermentation. That's a point where bacteria can grow. We do all our cooling inside the cooker, and we keep our facility really cold." Heist holds that the sweet-mash process makes for smoother whiskeys at the high proofs he chooses for bottling, and they certainly taste smooth.

Recommended Bottles

VALUE

Wilderness Trail Kentucky Straight High Rye Bourbon Bottled-in-Bond

Wilderness Trail Kentucky Straight Wheated Bourbon Bottled-in-Bond

SPECIAL OCCASION

Wilderness Trail Straight Rye Whiskey Bottled-in-Bond

Wilderness Trail Green Label Family Reserve Rye Barrel Select

Tasting Notes

WILDERNESS TRAIL KENTUCKY STRAIGHT HIGH RYE BOURBON BOTTLED-IN-BOND

64% corn, 24% rye, 12% malted barley; 5 to 7 years old; 50% ABV (100 proof)

It offers loads of vanilla with ripe apples, sweet baking spices, and some Red Hots. Oak and white pepper provide savory counterpoint before yielding to more vanilla and fruit on the finish.

WILDERNESS TRAIL KENTUCKY STRAIGHT WHEATED BOURBON BOTTLED-IN-BOND

64% corn, 26% wheat, 12% malted barley; 5 to 7 years old; 50% ABV (100 proof)

Light fruit and floral aromas with a little nutmeg and light brown sugar lead into multigrain cereal with brown sugar and dried apples on the palate. The finish runs long and tastes pleasantly oaky.

Casey Jones Distillery

Founded in 2014

CaseyJonesDistillery.com
2815 Witty Lane
Hopkinsville, KY 42240

During Prohibition, Alfred "Casey" Jones established a reputation for making quality still equipment prized by moonshiners making illegal whiskey. He did some moonshining himself, but after two stints in the big house and a warning that a third conviction would result in a life sentence, he "retired" from distilling to focus exclusively on making the equipment. Partakers of spirits made in the Jones-designed still considered them high quality, attributing the good taste, at least in part, to the still's unique design. Instead of the familiar rounded shape, its base consisted of a copper cube, making it easy to transport in a truck or wagon without tipping over.

These days, Arlon Casey Jones, Alfred's grandson, makes spirits legally and has updated his grandfather's design. At the new family facility—accessed by a narrow gravel road not always in the best condition, so leave the Duesenberg at home—he handcrafted the current still and all the woodwork. Tours offer a close-up view of the distilling process and the still room decorated with black-and-white photos, including Casey Jones making whiskey in a secluded hideout and the prison where he served time for doing so. The tour also offers a bracing taste of the 120-proof, new-make whiskey straight off the still. Unlike many small distilleries that stopped selling new-make whiskey once their Bourbon had matured, Casey Jones continues to sell a moonshine, as befits its history, and produces a rye.

TOTAL ECLIPSE MOONSHINE AND BOURBON

To commemorate the solar eclipse that occurred in North America in 2017, Casey Jones made moonshine using corn sent to the Moon in cooperation with Austin Peay University and NASA. The white whiskey had a four-grain mash bill: 75 percent corn, 10 percent wheat, 10 percent rye, 5 percent malted barley. A second release of the 'shine, joined by Total Eclipse Bourbon, took place ahead of 2024's eclipse. Before that alignment of heavenly bodies, the distillery offered a box set that included 375-milliliter bottles of moonshine and Bourbon and two pairs of eclipse-viewing glasses.

Recommended Bottles

VALUE

Casey Jones Small Batch Kentucky Straight Bourbon Whiskey Mash Bill 1

Casey Jones Small Batch Kentucky Straight Bourbon Whiskey Mash Bill 2

Casey Jones Total Eclipse Kentucky Straight Bourbon

SPECIAL OCCASION

Casey Jones Small Batch Wheated Kentucky Straight Bourbon Mash Bill 3

cask-strength expressions, any

Tasting Notes

CASEY JONES SMALL BATCH KENTUCKY STRAIGHT BOURBON WHISKEY MASH BILL 1

*96% corn, 3% rye, 1% malted barley;
at least 2 years old; 45% ABV (90 proof)*

Expect light notes of ripe apple and sweet corn with a pinch of cinnamon sugar. It has impressive balance and depth of flavor for a young whiskey. A drop or two of water elicits a little milk chocolate.

Castle & Key Distillery

Founded in 2014

CastleandKey.com
4445 McCracken Pike
Frankfort, KY 40601

Legendary distiller Colonel Edmund H. Taylor Jr. started his career as a banker before owning what has become the Buffalo Trace Distillery in Frankfort (page 3), on the banks of the Kentucky River. In 1887, beside Glenns Creek, he opened his Old Taylor Distillery, taking design inspiration from Europe. Resembling a Roman bath, a columned pavilion covers the keyhole-shaped reservoir holding spring water for the whiskey. At the entrance to the distillery, the stone office building evoked a crenellated castle, and the grounds featured a sunken garden like the one at Windsor Castle. Taylor knew that appearances matter, so he created a distillery as showpiece, making him a pioneer of Bourbon tourism. The site even included its own train station and a hotel. Period photographs show parties on the grounds attended by men in top hats and tailcoats and women in bustled dresses, holding parasols. Lore holds that Taylor himself owned more than 100 bespoke suits cut from the best Italian wool and tailored in New York City.

Later in life, Taylor parlayed his business success into politics, serving in Kentucky's House of Repre-

sentatives and Senate and serving as mayor of Frankfort for 16 years. He made fine whiskey, but sadly, that couldn't stop Prohibition from forcing the operation to close. After Repeal, the site reopened under the ownership of National Distillers, but the Bourbon slump forced it to close again in 1972. The warehouses held aging whiskey for a couple of more decades, while, for a time, other buildings housed an antiques and flea market. But mostly the facility sat derelict, behind a vine-clogged, chain-link fence, for decades.

In 2014, friends Will Arvin and Wes Murray of Lexington, a hedge fund manager and attorney respectively, bought the property for $950,000 and embarked on a long and costly restoration. Previous owners had used asbestos to fireproof the buildings, and invasive plants were choking the once elegant gardens and grounds. As part of the restoration, Arvin and Murray installed a 17-inch stainless-steel gin still and a 24-inch Vendome copper column still for rye and Bourbon. From Brown-Forman, Marianne Barnes (now Eaves)—assistant master distiller under Chris Morris (page 77)—joined as the first distiller, and developed Castle & Key's first releases before departing, in 2019, to go into consulting. Today, Castle & Key contract-distills and ages other brands, including Penelope, Pinhook, and Cream of Kentucky.

Arvin and Murray hired nationally renowned Lexington landscape architect Jon Carloftis to restore the gardens. He revived the formal sunken garden and landscaped the grounds with native species and a garden of herbs that Castle & Key uses in its Harvest Seasonal Gin. After the eye-catching castle and pavilion, the most notable building on the grounds is an enormous warehouse that, almost as long as two football fields, can hold 33,000 barrels of aging whiskey. During visitor hours, the 113-acre grounds, which feature hiking paths, are open to the public at no charge.

Recommended Bottles

VALUE
Castle & Key Small Batch Bourbon
Castle & Key Restoration Rye Whiskey

SPECIAL OCCASION
Castle & Key Small Batch Wheated Bourbon

Tasting Notes

CASTLE & KEY SMALL BATCH BOURBON

72% white corn, 17% malted barley, 10% rye; 4 years old; 49% ABV (98 proof)
Aromas include breakfast cereal topped with sliced apples and peaches, with flavors of rich vanilla accompanied by peaches, some melon, and a touch of light oak. Well balanced, it has some pepper and oak on the finish.

CASTLE & KEY SMALL BATCH WHEATED BOURBON

73% white corn, 17% malted barley, 10% white wheat; 4 years old; 46% ABV (92 proof)
It evokes rising yeast rolls with baked apples and sweet cherries. Think: caramel dusted with some cinnamon sugar. A second layer reveals notes of lemon and orange peels. A velvety mouthfeel ties everything together nicely.

THE BOTTLED-IN-BOND ACT

In the 1880s and '90s, most Americans drank Bourbon and rye sold by rectifiers, dealers who sourced it from multiple distilleries. Some of the resulting products simply blended a bunch of whiskeys, whereas others included grain neutral spirits that stretched the whiskey but kept the proof high. Some rectifiers added flavorings and colorings, including caramel, prune juice, and tea. Some spirits sold as "Bourbon" contained no whiskey at all, just neutral spirits mixed with various flavors and colors.

Deeply concerned about the state of the industry, Colonel Taylor obsessively guarded the quality of his whiskey in particular and of Kentucky Bourbon in general. He contacted his friend John Carlisle, who was serving as secretary of the US Treasury under President Grover Cleveland and who had served as speaker of the House and in the Kentucky legislature. Taylor wanted federal legislation to protect the integrity of Bourbon.

After hearings found that rectifiers were adulterating most "Bourbon," Congress passed the Bottled-in-Bond Act, which President Cleveland signed into law in 1897. A form of quality control, it required that any whiskey labeled "bottled-in-bond" be made at one distillery in one distilling season—January to June or July to December—

aged for at least four years in a government-bonded warehouse overseen by a federal gauging agent, and bottled at 100 proof (50 percent ABV). Bottled-in-bond whiskey didn't have to be the greatest whiskey, but it had to be whiskey. That legislation, America's first federal consumer-protection law, set the stage for the Pure Food and Drug Act, passed in 1906, which safeguarded a wide range of foods and beverages.

▲ John G. Carlisle

Dueling Grounds Distillery

Founded in 2014

DuelingGroundsDistillery.com
208 Harding Road
Franklin, KY 42134

Marc Dottore ran the artist management division of Universal South Records before going out on his own to represent Kathy Mattea, an award-winning country singer; Cherish the Ladies, a Celtic supergroup; and others. In the early 2010s, he grew interested in starting a distillery. He already knew about brewing beer, which uses some of the same chemistry as Bourbon, so he took the six-day distilling course at Moonshine University in Louisville. There, he learned not only the full process of distillation but also the business side.

Despite the tongue-in-cheek name, Moonshine University is both real and absolutely legitimate with a faculty of distillers and other spirits professionals from Kentucky distilleries and beyond. For more information, visit MoonshineUniversity.com.

In Franklin, just north of the Tennessee state line, Dottore found property for sale. It lay not far from Linkumpinch Farm, the historic site of many duels in the early 1800s. Tennessee duelers who didn't want to face legal consequences for their illegal confrontations in the Volunteer State crossed into Kentucky to wield their pistols at dawn. One of them, Sam Houston, later became president of the Republic of Texas.

Leaning into that history, Dottore named his distillery Dueling Grounds, starting with a 25-gallon pot still. Today the distillery uses a 200-gallon pot still and features tours, a cocktail bar, gift shop, and, on weekends, a pizza kitchen. They also make an unaged whiskey, fruit-infused corn whiskeys, a barrel-aged gin, and a dry gin. Dottore still manages the careers of country music performers.

KENTUCKY DUELS

Between 1790 and 1865, at least 40 duels took place in Kentucky, despite state law banning the practice. In 1850, the state legislature amended the state constitution so that no one who had participated in a duel could hold elective office. To this day, every state official and each person who passes the Kentucky bar exam must swear an oath that "I, _____, being a citizen of this state, have not fought a duel with deadly weapons within this state nor out of it, nor have I sent or accepted a challenge to fight a duel with deadly weapons, nor have I acted as a second in carrying a challenge, nor aided or assisted any person thus offending, so help me God." Kentucky remains the only state that requires its office holders and attorneys to verify that they haven't fought a duel.

Recommended Bottles

SPECIAL OCCASION
Linkumpinch Bourbon Bottled-in-Bond
Linkumpinch Single Barrel Bourbon Cask Strength

Tasting Notes

LINKUMPINCH BOURBON BOTTLED-IN-BOND

66% corn, 22% red winter wheat, 12% malted barley; 4 years old; 50% ABV (100 proof)

It features sweet and spicy notes of cinnamon, cardamom, and allspice balanced with orange Creamsicle and some caramel apple sprinkled with crushed nuts. The long finish concludes with a little chocolate before landing on some oak and pepper.

LINKUMPINCH SINGLE BARREL BOURBON CASK STRENGTH

66% corn, 22% red winter wheat, 12% malted barley; 4 years old; 61.3% ABV (122.6 proof), varies by batch

It has aromas of vanilla cream with cinnamon sugar, some apple, and sweet oak. Flavors of milk chocolate play around the edges and gradually fade as the peppery finish takes over. Add a little water for apples to rule the glass.

Second Sight Spirits

Founded in 2014

SecondSightSpirits.com
301 Elm Street
Ludlow, KY 41016

As high school freshmen, Rick Couch and Carus Waggoner spent hours after class tinkering in their parents' garages. Couch went to college to become a mechanical engineer; Waggoner, to study industrial design. They wanted to own their own shop, but until that happened, "We started taking on side gigs so we could either buy a new tool or learn a new technique," recalls Waggoner. Those side gigs turned into designing and building sets for acts in Las Vegas, including Cirque du Soleil and Siegfried and Roy. Eventually Couch and Waggoner wound up back in northern Kentucky, across the Ohio River from Cincinnati, where they started Second Sight Spirits.

Not surprisingly, they built the distillery themselves and put a showbiz spin on it with a fortune-telling theme. On a stage, the hybrid pot still sits behind a gold proscenium arch. Its shape resembles a cross-legged swami with the dome shaped like a turban. In the fermentation room, the doors to the spirits storage closets bear the names Spengler and Venkman, a nod to the Ghostbusters franchise. The main room of the coffee bar—a favorite gathering place for neighborhood residents—features a mural of a large hand with lines diagrammed for palm reading. Over the mantelpiece of an ornamental fireplace sits an aquarium, home to Fortuna the goldfish, which, in response to questions, swims in front of a panel of answers. "Wherever she hangs out, the background is your answer," Waggoner explains. "She's 100 percent not accurate."

Tours conclude with a tasting of several of Second Sights spirits, which, in addition to Bourbon, include a variety of rums and a hazelnut liqueur.

Recommended Bottle

VALUE

Oak Eye Kentucky Bourbon Whiskey

Tasting Notes

In 15-gallon barrels, Oak Eye ages just long enough to qualify as straight (not stated on the label).

OAK EYE KENTUCKY BOURBON WHISKEY

72% corn, 16% wheat, 7% malted barley, 5% rye; 2.1 years old; 46% ABV (92 proof) Nicely balanced, it smells of multigrain cereal sprinkled with brown sugar and vanilla, notes that carry onto the palate with some berries and cinnamon leading to a sweet oak finish.

New Riff Distilling

Founded in 2014

NewRiffDistilling.com
24 Distillery Way
Newport, KY 41073

Ken Lewis owned and managed several successful liquor stores in Kentucky for decades before deciding to start his own distillery. At the time, he owned the Party Source, one of the largest liquor stores in America. Kentucky law prohibits the owner of a liquor store from owning a distillery, though, so Lewis sold Party Source to his employees. With the proceeds, he built New Riff on the other side of the parking lot, just a couple of blocks from the Ohio River opposite Cincinnati. The sleek, modern facility features a 60-foot-tall copper column still enclosed in a glass tower that defines the building's exterior and looks especially striking when lit at night. In the rooftop bar, you can enjoy flights, cocktails, and small plates either after a tour or after work.

Lewis intended to create a "great small distillery," releasing all his Bourbons and ryes as bottled-in-bond. The law requires bottled-in-bond whiskey to age for at least four years, so the first New Riff release, a Bourbon, came from MGP. Lewis dubbed it O.K.I.,

which stood for "loved in Ohio, bottled in Kentucky, made in Indiana."

In 2023, Lewis retired, and his responsibilities passed to his daughter, Mollie Lewis, now company president, and to Hannah Lowen, New Riff's CEO. Lowen likes that New Riff, a second-generation company, plans to stay independent. In 2024, the company celebrated its 10th anniversary, and she sees longer-aged whiskeys in the coming years. "We've always saved about a third of what we produce to get older. We used to make 2,000 barrels a year. Now, we're closer to 6,000. These are aging both in warehouses next to our distillery and at our West Newport campus." Because of their urban location and highly flammable contents, the three warehouses in East Newport consist of concrete, instead of the more traditional wood, and contain fire-suppressant systems. Private barrel selections take place there.

Lowen situated the third New Riff property in Silver Grove, about 8 miles outside the city, where a trio of 40,000-barrel warehouses are starting to fill. "We've got enough capacity out there to get to homeostasis for our long-term, strategic plan to stay a big, small distillery."

In addition to whiskeys, New Riff makes two gins, both with Kentucky-grown botanicals. One of them ages in ex-whiskey barrels.

Recommended Bottles

VALUE

New Riff Kentucky Straight Bourbon

SPECIAL OCCASION

New Riff Single Barrel Kentucky Straight Bourbon
New Riff 8 Year Old Kentucky Straight Bourbon
New Riff Kentucky Straight Rye
New Riff Single Barrel Kentucky Straight Rye
New Riff Balboa Rye

Tasting Notes

New Riff non-chill filters its whiskeys, which means that some flavors from the distillation and aging remain after filtering. Adding cold water or ice may turn the whiskeys cloudy or hazy.

NEW RIFF KENTUCKY STRAIGHT BOURBON

65% corn, 30% rye, 5% malted barley; at least 4 years old; 50% ABV (100 proof)
You'll find butterscotch and herbal spices on the nose with a tingle of oak. On the palate, it has a rich, round mouthfeel and tastes of vanilla sugar cookie sprinkled with cinnamon and a pinch of clove. The complex flavors fade together, ending in dark fruit.

NEW RIFF SINGLE BARREL KENTUCKY STRAIGHT BOURBON

65% corn, 30% rye, 5% malted barley; at least 4 years old; 55.5 to 67% ABV (111 to 114 proof), varies by barrel
Barrel proof makes this a more muscular version of the bottled-in-bond Bourbon, with even more baking spices and some rich caramel. The fruit here leans toward cherries and plums, which come forward with a little water.

HEAD DISTILLER BRIAN SPRANCE

Before he came to New Riff, Brian Sprance had extensive brewing experience at Barrel House Brewing and Boston Beer Company. The name for fermentation liquid is "distiller's beer" because technically it *is* beer, after all. Sprance enjoys producing limited-release whiskeys that use special malts or percentages of malt not usually found in American whiskeys. Past expressions include Maltster Kentucky Straight Bourbon, made with crystal malt and malted rye; Backsetter Peated Backset Straight Rye, with some backset smoked using peat and 5 percent malted rye in the mash bill; and Kentucky Straight Malted Rye, made entirely with malted rye.

Boone County Distilling Company

Founded in 2015

MadeByGhosts.com
10601 Toebben Drive
Independence, KY 41051

In 1838, William Snyder of Albermarle County, Virginia, bought the stream mill in Petersburg, Kentucky, taking advantage of the location on a bend in the Ohio River to build the Petersburg Distillery. Over the decades, production grew, and ownership changed. By 1874, Julius Freiburg and Levi Workum of Cincinnati owned the facility, which had become one of the largest distilleries in the state, selling W. T. Snyder and Lexington Club Bourbons and Appleton and Boone County whiskeys.

At the turn of the 20th century, Peterburg's economy had faded. The Whiskey Trust, an organization that had conglomerated several distilleries, absorbed the Petersburg Distillery as well. With Prohibition, production ceased altogether. An added insult, the building served for a time as the Petersburg jail.

In 2015, Jack Wells and Josh Quinn, longtime friends and Boone County residents, decided to get into the Bourbon business and bring it back to the area. They opened their operation in a local industrial park—with a 500-gallon pot still named The Bear in honor of the pet bear that William Snyder walked around on a leash—sourced some Bourbon from MGP, and released it under the 1833 brand. Today, they offer Boone County Small Batch Bourbon, a series of Cask Finished Founder's Reserve Bourbons, Lexington Club, and White Hall Tavern Bourbon Cream.

Recommended Bottles

VALUE
Boone County Small Batch Bourbon

SPECIAL OCCASION
Founder's Reserve Amburana Cask Finished
  Kentucky Straight Bourbon Whiskey

Tasting Notes

**BOONE COUNTY SMALL
BATCH BOURBON**
*75% corn, 21% rye, 4% malted barley;
no age statement; 45.4% ABV
(90.8 proof)*
Fruity aromas include cherries and
apricots, which carry onto the palate,
where plenty of caramel and vanilla
support them. Baking spices, predomi-
nantly cinnamon, provide balance.
It finishes with a whisper of oak.

Neeley Family Distillery

Founded in 2015

NeeleyFamilyDistillery.com
4360 KY Hwy 1130
Sparta, KY 41086

Hailing from the mountains of Owsley County, southeast of Lexington, the Neeley family has a long history of mostly illegal distilling that begins 11 generations back with James Neeley, who made his first whiskey in about 1740. Many of his descendants continued making and selling untaxed whiskey, which became known as "moonshine" only during Prohibition. Moonshiners hid their stills in forested mountains, away from the prying eyes of revenuers, and plied their art at night, when they could see by the light of the moon. But gov-ernment agents weren't their only adversaries. Disputes with other illegal distilleries arose, too.

Far easier to find than previous whiskey-making operations, the completely legal Neeley Family Distillery includes an exhibit that covers much of that history. Highlights include vintage moonshining stills and a rifle that an adversary used to murder a great-great-grandfather of current and legal distiller Royce Neeley. It came into the Neeley family because Leonard Neeley, Royce's great-grandfather, killed the murderer and took the rifle as a trophy.

The distillery—in a handsome log structure built by Roy Neeley, Royce's father, who eschewed distilling to become a builder—houses a pair of custom-made pot stills. When Royce Neeley revived the family's distilling tradition, he resumed many of his forefathers' techniques, too. For fermentation, he captures wild yeast. Rather than using the common sour-mash technique—which takes backset from the previous fermentation to start the next one—he employs the sweet-mash method, which begins each fermentation anew. The distillery also makes absinthe and, given the family heritage, several expressions of moonshine, both unflavored and flavored.

HIDDEN BARN

In 2022, Jackie Zykan, former master taster for Old Forester (page 15), collaborated with Neeley Family Distillery to create Hidden Barn, a small-batch Bourbon blended from 4 to 22 barrels. The name refers to the practice, in rural communities, of hiding illegal stills in barns. *Baudoinia compniacensis*, also called whiskey fungus or distillery fungus, feeds on evaporating alcohol and coats nearby surfaces. The black fungus stained the walls of the barns, so to protect the moonshiners,

everyone painted their barns black to hide telltale evidence of the illegal activity from authorities. Several Hidden Barn batches release each year. Flavor profiles vary considerably from batch to batch, though many taste grain-forward. Several expressions feature a black label.

Tasting Notes

NEELEY FAMILY DISTILLERY BOURBON

67% corn, 25% rye, 18% malted barley; 28 months old; 53.3% ABV (106.5 proof)

Expect maple syrup, apricots, and baking spices on the nose. The palate exhibits canned peaches, caramel, nuts, and some new leather with cinnamon and a pinch of pepper.

NEELEY FAMILY DISTILLERY SINGLE BARREL

64% corn, 38% wheat, 8% malted barley; 19 months old; 50.3% ABV (100.6 proof)

The distillery rotates the grain recipes and proofs of its single-barrel selection. At any given time, the gift shop carries three, differentiated by the mash bills. This one begins with aromas of pecans, brown sugar, some light fruit, and milk chocolate. On the palate, it becomes more fruity with vanilla, berries, and plums, drying to pepper and oak.

Recommended Bottle

Other worthwhile expressions include R. D. R. Neeley Sweet Thumped Kentucky Straight Rye Whiskey and Old Jett Brothers Kentucky Straight Bourbon, a series of releases finished in ex-wine and other spirits barrels.

VALUE
Neeley Family Distillery Bourbon
Neeley Family Distillery Single Barrel

SPLURGE
Hidden Barn

Bardstown Bourbon Company

Founded in 2016

BardstownBourbon.com
1500 Parkway Drive
Bardstown, KY 40004

In the mid-2010s, former telecom executive Peter Loftin, like so many other Bourbon lovers, wanted to start his own brand. The easiest way to do that is to buy whiskey from a large distillery, and plenty of people had the same idea, putting sourced whiskey in high demand. He decided to build his own distillery. Like the Shapira brothers, who started Heaven Hill in the 1930s (page 45), Loftin had no experience as a distiller himself, so he hired one. Steve Nally—Donna's husband (page xv), former master distiller at Maker's Mark, and a member of the Kentucky Bourbon Hall of Fame—agreed to exit retirement in 2016 to head Loftin's new distilling team.

Bardstown Bourbon Company (BBC) set a mission not only to make its own whiskey but also to partner with other brands in collaborative distilling. That practice means using the mash bills and yeast strains specified by the clients, not the contract distiller, and BBC was up and running just in time to meet demand that Loftin hadn't expected. Almost immediately, the business was devoting about 90 percent of its production to other brands and running out of capacity.

> Ethan Spalding, Steve Nally's grandson, serves as the distiller at the Buzzard's Roost Whiskey Row experience in Louisville (page 201). Buzzard's Roost ages and bottles its whiskeys at BBC.

"In September 2016, there was one 36-inch column still," recalls Dan Callaway, vice president for product development. "It ran 24 hours a day. Then we added another 36-inch still, and that's how we got to 7.3 million gallons. We just added a 42-inch column still, so now we're at more than 10 million gallons annually." To put that in perspective, Four Roses, one of the nine legacy distilleries in Kentucky, makes about 8 million gallons per year.

▲ Steve Nally, head of Bardstown's distilling team

According to Callaway, the current ratio of collaborations to BBC whiskey proper sits at about 80/20. Demand remains strong, and BBC continues collaborating in other ways. The bar at the distillery, with shelves reaching to the high ceiling, stocks Bourbons and ryes from most of the other Kentucky distilleries. The cocktail program includes the classics and creative drinks such as Bourbon milkshakes, almost whole meals in themselves. The Kitchen & Bar restaurant, which occupies most of the lobby inside the entrance, offers a view of the still room and features an "elevated Southern" menu, including a Kentucky country ham tasting, buttermilk fried chicken sandwich, and ravioli stuffed with Kentucky lamb.

BBC's expansion has included property and warehouses as well. The original campus covered 100 acres. Across the road, another 300 joined the fold in order to add 13 more warehouses to the existing 17. As distilling capacity has expanded, so have visitor experiences. In addition to the basic one-hour tour, you can take a special tour with master distiller Steve Nally, visit a rickhouse to thieve Bourbon from a trio of barrels, fill your own bottles, take a cocktail class, and enjoy a curated food-and-whiskey pairing.

Recommended Bottles

BBC's core portfolio consists of the Origin Series, always available at the distillery and at retailers that stock the brand. Two other series have two releases each year. The Discovery Series features special blends of whiskeys produced at BBC and other distilleries. The Collaborative Series showcases BBC whiskey aged in secondary barrels that held other spirits, wine, or beer. These finishes vary with each release.

VALUE

Origin Series Kentucky Straight Bourbon
Origin Series Kentucky Straight Bourbon
  Bottled-in-Bond

SPLURGE

Discovery Series, any
Collaborative Series, any

Tasting Notes

BARDSTOWN BOURBON COMPANY ORIGIN SERIES KENTUCKY STRAIGHT BOURBON

60% corn, 36% rye, 4% malted barley; 6 years old; 48% ABV (96 proof)

Smooth with a rich mouthfeel, it tastes sweet, like orange marmalade, some vanilla, new saddle leather, and a bit of oak. Some cinnamon, nutmeg, and a pinch of pepper balance that sweetness.

BARDSTOWN BOURBON COMPANY ORIGIN SERIES KENTUCKY STRAIGHT BOURBON BOTTLED-IN-BOND

68% corn, 20% wheat, 12% malted barley; 6 years old; 50% ABV (100 proof)

The wheat in the mash bill emerges in aromas and flavors of coffee cake sprinkled with nuts and fruit. It leans heavily toward the vanilla side of the Bourbon flavor spectrum with some sweet cream and a touch of honey.

BARDSTOWN BOURBON COMPANY DISCOVERY SERIES #11 (2024)

73% from 75% corn, 13% rye, 12% malted barley from Kentucky; 13 years old; 21% from 78% corn, 13% rye, 9% malted barley from Kentucky; 10 years old; 6% from 68% corn, 20% wheat, 12% malted barley produced at BBC; 6 year old; 59% ABV (118.1 proof)

Complex aromas include berries, cherries, toffee, and a whiff of smoke, Expect rich notes of cinnamon, dry fruits, vanilla pudding, and a pinch of pepper on the palate. It finishes with a tingle of alcohol-infused cherries and some leather.

Jeptha Creed Distillery

Founded in 2016

JepthaCreed.com
500 Gordon Lane
Shelbyville, KY 40065

Bruce Nethery farms land in Shelby County, Kentucky, which his family has owned for five generations. He took pride in that pedigree but also wanted to make Bourbon. He didn't have any distilling experience, though, and, other than Shelbyville and drinks by the glass in restaurants, the county had voted itself dry after Prohibition. A distillery could make whiskey there, but it couldn't offer tastings or sell alcohol in its gift shop.

It just so happened that Joyce Nethery, Bruce's wife, earned degrees in chemical engineering, a background now common among distillers. She happily helped her husband realize his dream. Then, in 2018, Shelby County voted to allow sales of packaged alcohol throughout the jurisdiction.

Adjacent to I-64 between Louisville and Lexington, 64 acres of the Nethery property offered a perfect spot to build a distillery visible easily from the highway. The Netherys named it Jeptha Creed because the Jeptha Knobs—a series of peaks likely formed by a prehistoric asteroid impact and named by Daniel and Squire Boone after a judge of the ancient Israelites—bisected their farm. They added "Creed" as a company promise to uphold their shared values.

Painted bright red with black trim, the distillery resembles a large, architecturally distinguished barn. The fermenting mash catches the eye, too. Rather than the usual dark yellow, Jeptha Creed mash looks pink because it uses Bloody Butcher, an heirloom variety of corn that has dark red kernels. That corn

▼ Joyce and Autumn Nethery at Jeptha Creed Distillery

grows on the Nethery farm, making Jeptha Creed a ground-to-glass establishment.

Jeptha Creed first released a four-grain Bourbon that remains the heart of the portfolio. Red, White & Blue Straight Bourbon recently joined it and uses Bloody Butcher, an heirloom white corn, and a blue corn. The company donates part of the proceeds of that expression to not-for-profit organizations helping veterans.

The cocktail bar offers a wide array of drinks: flights of the distillery's products, traditional cocktails, and some just for fun, such as Bourbon slushies. Besides Bourbon, Jeptha Creed distills flavored vodkas, flavored moonshines, and fruit brandies sourced from the orchard on the property. The fruit for all Jeptha Creed's products comes from the

Autumn, the Netherys' daughter and a co-owner of the business, spent a year in Scotland, studying distilling. She now serves as the marketing manager for the company, making the business a family enterprise.

Nethery land as well, including blueberries, raspberries, and a variety of mints. As an integral part of the Shelbyville community, the distillery offers dedicated events spaces, and each summer, Jeptha Creed hosts Jammin' at Jeptha, a concert series showcasing the talents of a variety of country and bluegrass musicians.

Recommended Bottles

VALUE
Jeptha Creed Straight 4-Grain Bourbon

SPECIAL OCCASION
Jeptha Creed Red, White & Blue Straight Bourbon
Jeptha Creed Bottled-in-Bond Bourbon

Tasting Notes

JEPTHA CREED STRAIGHT 4-GRAIN BOURBON

70% Bloody Butcher corn, 15% malted rye, 10% malted wheat, 5% malted barley; no age statement; 49% ABV (98 proof)

Expect candy corn, ripe peaches, some vanilla, and brown sugar. It alternates between Halloween and peach cobbler, especially when the cinnamon appears, and finishes with a flourish of citrus and oak.

JEPTHA CREED RED, WHITE & BLUE STRAIGHT BOURBON

25% Bloody Butcher corn, 25% heirloom white corn, 25% blue corn, 10% malted barley; no age statement; 50% ABV (100 proof)

It begins with lots of vanilla followed by berries, peaches, orange peel, and baking spices. Some darker notes of coffee and chocolate make fleeting appearances that add depth and complexity. It ends with a pinch of pepper.

Augusta Distillery

Founded in 2018

AugustaKYDistillery.com
207 Seminary Avenue
Augusta, KY 41002

In 2017, Lance and Lalani Bates bought and renovated Augusta's historic Beehive Tavern overlooking the Ohio River. They also wanted to bring Kentucky's signature industry to their hometown, so they acquired a 40,000-square foot commercial building built in the early 1800s that once housed a carriage factory, among other businesses. In 2022, the distillery released its first whiskey, Buckner's Single Barrel, a sourced premium 13-year-old Bourbon named for Philip Buckner, the town's founder. Alex Castle joined as master distiller in 2024.

The pair of 32-foot, 14-inch Vendome column stills can produce about 14,000 barrels' worth of whiskey per year. Nonetheless, the facility remains a work in

progress, open for "pardon our dust" tours and tastings. Lance Bates has a bigger plan than just making what he calls "super-premium" Bourbons. "We wanted to provide what we call an ecosystem, a way to give back to the community and create sustainable economic opportunities. That was why we also wanted to have a restaurant. We have a bed and breakfast as well as horseback riding trails. We want people to come and spend the weekend." When complete in 2026 or 2027, the facility also will feature a full-service bar, an open-air space for concerts, and a dedicated area for food trucks.

If you visit Augusta, check out the Rosemary Clooney House, where the award-winning actress and singer lived when not in Beverly Hills. Open for tours, it includes exhibits of her costumes from *White Christmas* and other movies, as well some costumes of George Clooney, one of her nephews.

Recommended Bottles

SPLURGE

Old Route 8 Single Barrel Bourbon
Augusta Buckner's 10 Year Old

Tasting Notes

OLD ROUTE 8 SINGLE BARREL BOURBON

74% corn, 18% rye, 8% malted barley; 8 years old; 62.8% ABV (125.5 proof)

Very fruity and rich on the nose, it has aromas of raisins, vanilla custard, and some confectioners' sugar. The flavors feature a complex interplay of chocolate-covered cherries and vanilla caramels with a pinch of baking spices. The long finish ends in oak and a touch of spice.

▲ Thieving whiskey from the barrel

▲ Alex Castle, Augusta's master distiller

BAKER-BIRD WINERY AND B. BIRD DISTILLERY

In the 1700s, Johannes Becker emigrated from what later became Germany, changed his name to John Baker, and fought for the American colonies during the revolution. After the war, he came to Kentucky and started a distillery near Augusta. In the 1850s, Abraham Baker Jr., Baker's grandson, built the largest wine cellar in America that still exists today, a reminder that, before the Civil War, Kentucky ranked as the third-largest wine-producing state in the country. In 2018, Dinah Bird resumed distilling on the site. She makes about 400 cases of award-winning wine per year and is aging about 100 cases of Bourbon scheduled to release soon. If you visit Augusta Distillery, only a few minutes away, make time for a tour and some wine at this facility on the National Register of Historic Places. For more information, visit BakerBirdWineryDistillery.com

Lux Row Distillers

Founded in 2018

LuxRowDistillers.com
1 Lux Row
Bardstown, KY 40004

About three and a half miles east of downtown Bardstown once stood the historic Ballard family farm. Listed on the National Register of Historic Places, a handsome stone house from 1806 remains. Today the property hosts Lux Row Distillery. The modern facility resembles a barn, with tall glass windows and even a faux silo. But Lux Row's roots lie in St. Louis, Missouri.

David Sherman started his eponymous liquor distribution company there in 1958. Renamed LuxCo in 2006, its portfolio included sangria, liqueurs, Tequilas, and a handful of Bourbons that Heaven Hill was contract-distilling at the time. When the Bourbon category started growing again, Heaven Hill needed to pivot its resources to producing its own whiskeys. So LuxCo's husband-and-wife team, Donn and Michele Lux, built their own distillery in Kentucky.

Master distiller John Rempe oversees the production of several whiskeys, some already LuxCo brands—Ezra Brooks, Rebel, David Nicholson, Blood Oath—and a couple of brands that originated with the new distillery: Daviess County and Lux Row. The old stone house—which, some say, ghosts haunt—contains a handsome bar where, after a tour, you can enjoy tastings, cocktails, and private barrel selections. From the property's previous owners, Lux Row inherited the resident flock of peacocks, a feature you'll find at no other Kentucky distillery.

▲ John Rempe, master distiller at Lux Row

A STITZEL-WELLER CONNECTION

In the 1930s, the Rebel Yell brand originated at Julian Van Winkle's Stitzel-Weller Distillery in Louisville (page 53), intended to appeal specifically to the southern market. Like all Bourbons produced there, it contained wheat instead of rye. Today's incarnation, Rebel, distances itself from association with the Confederacy. The old label featuring a gray-coated, saber-wielding soldier astride a galloping horse has given way to the slogan: "Defiantly Smooth Wheated Bourbon."

Recommended Bottles

BARGAIN
Ezra Brooks 99 Proof
Rebel Kentucky Straight Bourbon Whiskey

VALUE
David Nicholson 1843

SPECIAL OCCASION
Lux Row Distillery Bourbon

SPLURGE
Old Ezra 7 Year Bourbon
Blood Oath (limited releases)

Tasting Notes

EZRA BROOKS 99 PROOF

78% corn, 12% malted barley, 10% rye; no age statement; 49.5% ABV (99 proof)
It has a surprisingly light nose for the proof, with touches of vanilla, mint, and sugar cookie. But substantial flavors emerge from the rich mouthfeel: caramel, green peppercorns, vanilla pudding, nuts, and leather.

REBEL KENTUCKY STRAIGHT BOURBON WHISKEY

wheated (mash bill not released), no age statement, 50% ABV (100 proof)
It smells like baking biscuits, with some light notes of vanilla and orange zest. Some honey, brown sugar, and almonds join those aromas on the palate.

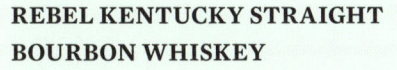

DAVID NICHOLSON 1843

mash bill not released, no age statement, 50% ABV (100 proof)
It imparts lots of corn and vanilla on the nose, with some orange zest and a whiff of banana. The palate exhibits some caramel corn with a bit of vanilla and black pepper. Ultimately it tastes herbal rather than fruity.

Preservation Distillery

Founded in 2018

PreservationDistillery.com
426 Sutherland Road
Bardstown, KY 40004

Marci Palatella's somewhat unlikely involvement in Kentucky Bourbon came via her California wine-exporting business. "In the 1980s, when Bourbon wasn't a thing, I helped many distributors who had warehouses full of old Bourbon, stuff that they'd been sitting on for years, sell it." Some of that "stuff" included Bourbons for which today's collectors would pay top dollar, such as 1960s Christmas expressions of I. W. Harper.

Palatella had willing buyers in Europe and especially in Japan. After she had sold the old, sourced whiskeys, her customers wanted to know what else she had. In response, she came up with Very Olde St. Nick, a series of Bourbons and ryes sourced and blended from old stock. (Today's Very Olde St. Nick also includes some whiskey pot-distilled at Preservation.)

As Bourbon once again became popular, the demand for older whiskeys grew. Palatella decided to make whiskeys with the same rich, complex character of those that she had been selling. She sought advice from Even Kulsveen, who successfully had revived Willett Distillery (page 57) to produce premium Bourbons and ryes. In 2015, Palatella purchased a derelict tobacco farm outside Bardstown that she transformed into Preservation Distillery.

The main complex consists of three barns painted white with dark trim. In the middle, the distillery contains a pair of custom pot stills. Another barn serves as the Guest House, meaning visitor center. The third, formerly an event space, now hosts private barrel selections. Embracing sustainability, Palatella had two wells drilled 200 feet through the limestone beneath the farm for water. On the property, she installed a herd of longhorn cattle, and a silhouette of a longhorn's head forms part of the company logo. "They graze, we have organic hay that we grow here for them, and they eat the spent mash from our distilling." Preservation sources the corn for the whiskey locally.

Preservation makes ultra-premium spirits that cost more than $100 per bottle and many more than $200. At the end of a tour, you can taste a selection of what's available. Almost all expressions come from single barrels or single batches of two or three barrels. Limited editions are by design, no two ever taste alike. Wattie Boone & Sons, one of the brands, comes from Tennessee and nods to Walter Boone—perhaps a distant relative of famous pioneer Daniel—who, records show, was distilling on Beech Fork River, which runs along the Preservation Farm, in 1776. In 2024, the distillery reached a milestone with the release of Preservation Bourbon, its own whiskey made using a wheated mash bill, fermented with a combination of cultured yeast and wild yeast captured on the farm, and aged for six and a half years.

A VAN WINKLE CONNECTION

Marci Palatella's husband, Lou, had worked in the whiskey industry. When she was sourcing old whiskey, he told her that, early in his career, he knew a man who made great whiskey and that, after he died, his son had taken over the business. Now his grandson was running the company, which might make a good source for the dusties that she was hunting.

The grandson was Julian Van Winkle III (page ix), and he happily let Palatella sell his Old Rip Van Winkle Bourbon. She told him that her husband had known his grandfather, known affectionately as "Pappy" in the family, and had many stories about him. "I called Julian and told him that he should make a Pappy [Bourbon]," she says, "and he thought I was out of my mind." He didn't think anyone cared about his grandfather. But Van Winkle found a photo of his grandfather smoking a cigar, which became the basis of the labels for the now legendary Pappy Van Winkle brand.

Recommended Bottles

SPLURGE

Preservation
Very Olde St. Nick
Rare Perfection
Wattie Boone & Sons
Pure Antique
Old Man Winter

Tasting Notes

VERY OLDE ST. NICK 'IMMACULATA' ANCIENT CASK BOURBON, 2023

mash bill not released, no age statement (blended with a 15-year-old base) 59% ABV (118.1 proof)
Layered and complex, it suggests spiced cherries, pear, raisins, apple, orange peel, allspice, new leather, blackberry preserves, and sweet oak, all imbedded in a rich base of toffee and roasted nuts. The luscious mouthfeel results in a finish that doesn't want to end.

Log Still Distillery

Founded in 2022

LogStillDistillery.com
225 Dee Head Road
Gethsemane, KY 40051

In the late 1800s, near Gethsemane Station on the Louisville and Nashville Railroad line, Joseph Bernard Dant built and operated Cold Spring Distillery. It closed with Prohibition. After Repeal, his son William Washington Dant and business partner Joe B. Head rebuilt on the site and opened the Dant & Head Distillery. They sold it in 1940, and it passed through a series of owners until the facility closed in 1961.

Perched above abandoned buildings in various states of decay, the rusting water tower became something of a local landmark, which Charles Dant, who grew up nearby, remembers climbing as a kid. When growing up, cousin Lynne Dant recalled conversations among her family that always seemed to end with: "Why did Granddaddy sell the distillery?" or "Sure wish he hadn't gotten out of the Bourbon business."

In 2019, Wally Dant, another cousin, bought the land and ruins, returning the Dant family to the Bourbon business. He invited Lynne, a chemical engineer, to serve as COO and distiller of Log Still Distillery, and Charles to oversee the 350-acre campus, including a 12-acre lake, as VP of operations. (Lynne left in 2024.)

"We take water from that spring," Wally explains, pointing uphill, "pump it up to the distillery, and use that spring water as our cut water for our barrels and bottling," which continues the family tradition.

The main distillery features a 33-foot-tall column still made by Vendome with an unusual customization. The outer covering resembles the bark of a poplar tree. When aged, poplar wood becomes almost stone hard. In the 1700s, many of Kentucky's farmer-distillers who couldn't afford copper stills distilled in hollowed poplar logs fitted with copper piping. The name of Log Still acknowledges that history. A new building houses the microdistillery—which contains a 50-gallon Vendome hybrid pot still that develops new products and which features a special distill-your-own program for guests—and the tasting room.

The Dants sourced the Monk's Road Bourbons currently available. Their own distilled whiskeys will hit shelves no earlier than 2026 because they won't release a product that has aged for fewer than four years. From Bardstown to Log Still, Monks Road runs past the Abbey of Gethsemane, where Thomas Merton, Trappist monk and author of *The Seven Story Mountain* lived and wrote from 1941 to 1968. The distillery produces a citrus-forward London Dry Monk's Road Gin and a Monk's Road Barrel Finished Gin aged in ex-Bourbon barrels. It also sources Tennessee whiskey sold under the Rattle & Snap brand.

The Dants refurbished the old water tower and converted four houses on the grounds into bed-and-breakfast accommodations. A 2,000-seat amphitheater features mostly country music headliners for weekend concerts from May through October. Past acts have included Billy Ray Cyrus, Wynonna Judd, and Alabama. A 20,000-square-foot events venue contains a banquet hall and wedding chapel. The tiny Gethsemane Depot train station sits by the railroad tracks that still run through the property.

"We've got walking trails. We've got fishing—bass, bluegill, catfish—and we've hooked up with the Kentucky Railroad Museum," Charles Dant explains. "They've got two overnight cars, a presidential car that sleeps three couples, and a nice dining car."

Recommended Bottles

In addition to its wheated Small Batch expression, Log Still releases the Fifth District Series, named after Kentucky's fifth whiskey tax district, which, before Prohibition, contained more than 100 distilleries across 17 counties.

VALUE
Monk's Road Small Batch Bourbon

Tasting Notes

Log Still doesn't release the mash bills for any of its expressions.

MONK'S ROAD SMALL BATCH BOURBON

4 years old, 47% ABV (94 proof)
It evokes ripe berries with light vanilla and light brown sugar. A honey note sweetens and smooths it, and a pinch of green peppercorn drying to a pop of oak on the finish provides balance.

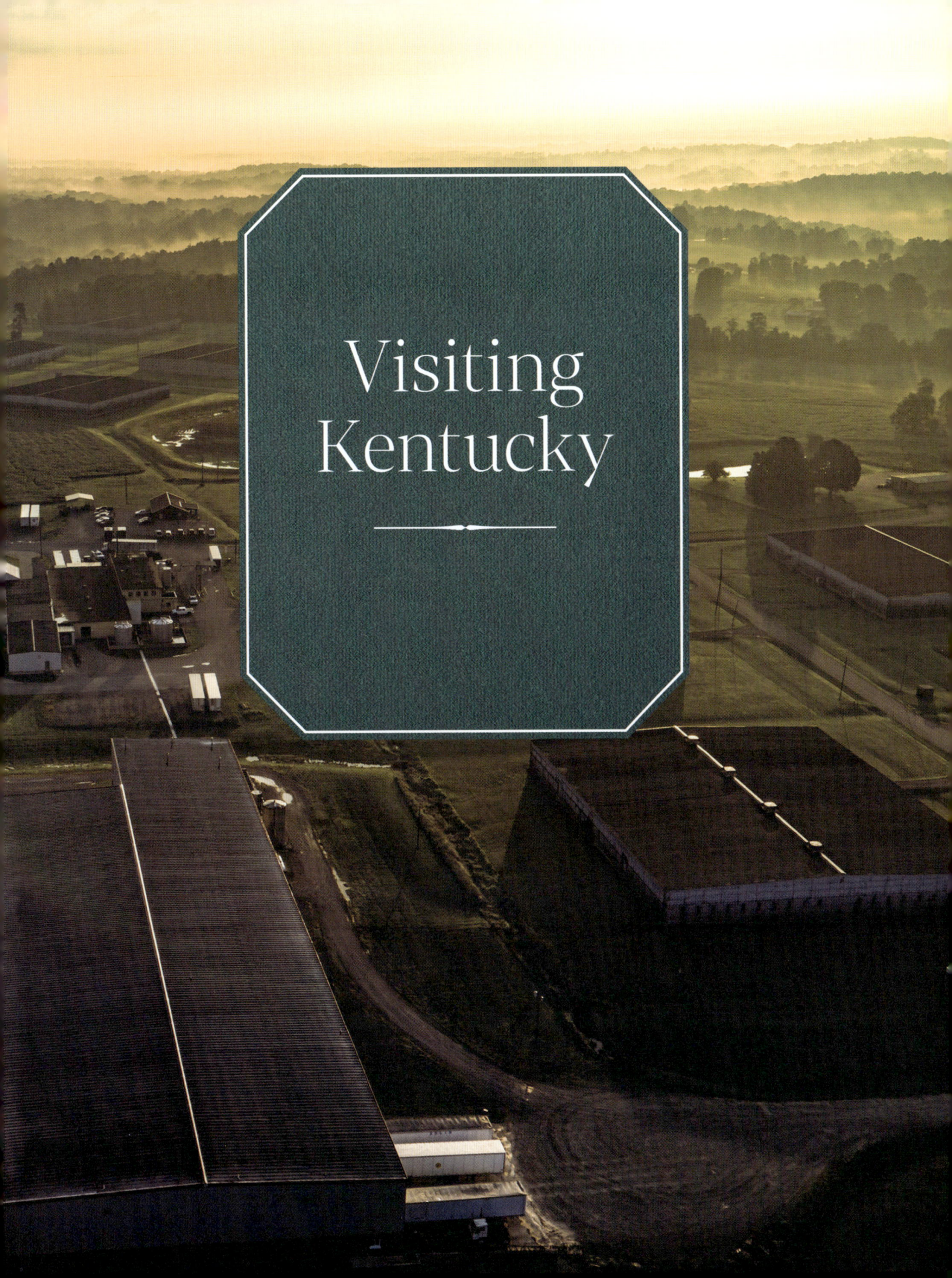

Visiting
Kentucky

RYE   MALTED
       BARLEY

HOPPER

FEED ROLLER

HAMMERS

TO COOKING

▲ Louisville Distilling Company on Main Street, Louisville

Louisville's Whiskey Row

Before Prohibition, more than 80 Bourbon-related businesses lined Louisville's Main Street, which became known as Whiskey Row. The companies included metalworks that made parts for stills and other equipment, whiskey warehouses, sales offices for most of the state's distilleries, liquor wholesalers, saloons, railroad offices for overland distribution, shipping companies that transported Bourbon up and down the Ohio and Mississippi Rivers, and publishing offices of the *Wine and Spirits Bulletin*. All this Bourbon-related commerce earned Main Street the nickname "the Wall Street of Whiskey." Perhaps ironically, the street had no working distilleries on it.

Today, Whiskey Row consists of a stretch of 10 city blocks containing several working distilleries, tasting rooms and whiskey workshops, bars and restaurants emphasizing Bourbon and Bourbon cocktails, and other whiskey attractions. Built largely in the 1800s, blocks of structures, four to seven stories tall, line both sides of the street, forming the largest collection of buildings with cast-iron and stone facades in America outside the SoHo neighborhood of downtown Manhattan. Interspersed with whiskey attractions, many of these buildings contain restaurants, museums, shops, hotels, and offices. If you visit, look for tall, yellow-and-black markers along the sidewalks

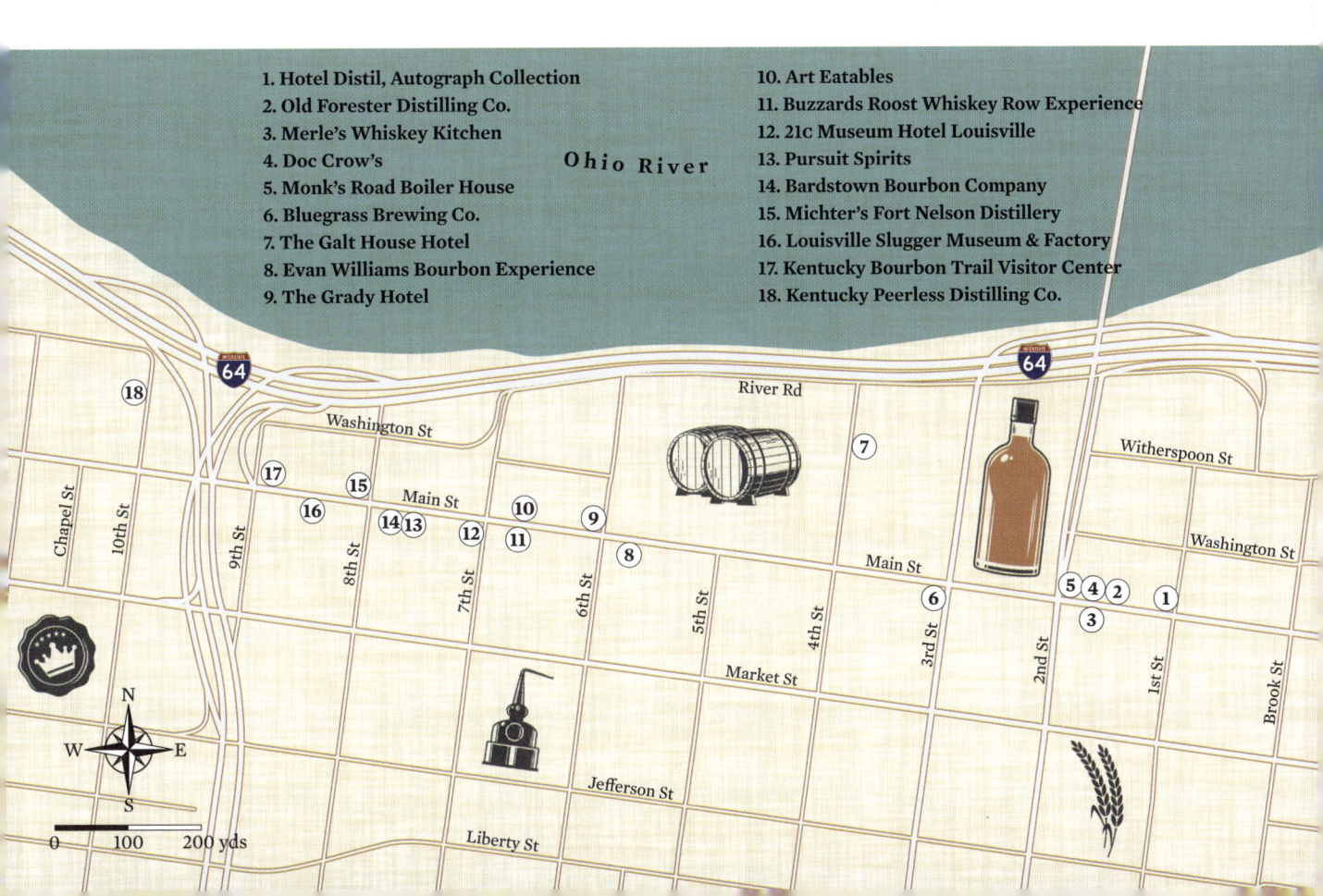

1. Hotel Distil, Autograph Collection
2. Old Forester Distilling Co.
3. Merle's Whiskey Kitchen
4. Doc Crow's
5. Monk's Road Boiler House
6. Bluegrass Brewing Co.
7. The Galt House Hotel
8. Evan Williams Bourbon Experience
9. The Grady Hotel
10. Art Eatables
11. Buzzards Roost Whiskey Row Experience
12. 21c Museum Hotel Louisville
13. Pursuit Spirits
14. Bardstown Bourbon Company
15. Michter's Fort Nelson Distillery
16. Louisville Slugger Museum & Factory
17. Kentucky Bourbon Trail Visitor Center
18. Kentucky Peerless Distilling Co.

Ohio River

that detail the Bourbon businesses that used to operate at those locations in the late 1800s and early 1900s. Set in the concrete in front of the doors of each building, address markers also name long-vanished businesses that once occupied those storefronts.

The following list runs from east to west.

HOTEL DISTIL, AUTOGRAPH COLLECTION
101 West Main Street
marriott.com/en-us/hotels/
sdfak-hotel-distil-autograph-collection/overview
This Bourbon-themed hotel features luxuriously appointed rooms, a rooftop bar, and the Repeal Oak-Fired Steakhouse, which boasts a large, well-curated whiskey list and many vintage bottles. At check-in, each hotel guest receives a "prescription" (voucher) for a drink in the lobby at 7:33 p.m. (19:33 in 24-hour time) in honor of the year of Repeal.

OLD FORESTER DISTILLING COMPANY
117–119 West Main Street
OldForester.com/distillery
See page 9.

MERLE'S WHISKEY KITCHEN
122 West Main Street
MerlesWhiskeyKitchen.com
Southern and southwestern flavors dominate the menu with candied Bourbon maple bacon, fried chicken, guacamole, nachos, pulled pork, tacos, and more. The establishment also serves cocktails and local craft beers on tap and has a 150-bottle whiskey list that includes the restaurant's private barrel selections. Live bluegrass, country, and honky-tonk music play nightly.

**DOC CROW'S SOUTHERN
SMOKEHOUSE AND RAW BAR**
127 West Main Street
DocCrows.com
Smoked meats, fried green tomatoes, po'boys, and
oysters on the half shell anchor the menu at this
casual, atmospheric eatery that also has a craft cocktail program, an excellent selection of draft beer, and
a whiskey menu featuring more than 2,500 different
bottles.

MONKS ROAD BOILER HOUSE
131 West Main Street
LogStillDistillery.com
This Louisville satellite for Log Still Distillery—
makers of whiskey and gin, located in Gethsemane,
Kentucky, south of Bardstown (page 193)—features a
tasting room, cocktail bar, and fine dining restaurant
with an emphasis on steak and seafood.

BLUEGRASS BREWING COMPANY
300 West Main Street
BBCBrew.com
Traditional American fare served at the city's oldest brewpub includes chicken wings, burgers, pork
chops, and pizzas. The beer list includes a stout aged
in Four Roses barrels, and Bluegrass has a good
Bourbon list. The third-floor Bourbon Barrel Loft
hosts private events.

GALT HOUSE HOTEL
140 North 4th Street at West Main Street
GaltHouse.com
Named for a much smaller 19th-century hotel that
stood at the corner of Second and Main Streets, this
giant riverfront hotel has more than 1,300 guest
rooms and suites and multiple conference spaces.
In 1972, Jockey Silks, the hotel bar, became the first
Bourbon bar to open in the city.

EVAN WILLIAMS BOURBON EXPERIENCE
528 West Main Street
EvanWilliams.com
In the late 1700s, Welsh immigrant Evan Williams
became one of the first commercial distillers in Kentucky, and his small distillery coincidentally stood
about a block north of this location. The Louisville
homeplace of this Heaven Hill brand (page 45) offers
tours of its microdistillery that produces one barrel
per day. On the second floor, tasting rooms and bars
recreate facades of pre-Prohibition Main Street. The
basement speakeasy hosts private events.

GRADY HOTEL
601 West Main Street
TheGradyHotel.com
This 1883 building once housed a pharmacy that dispensed Bourbon for a multitude of ailments. Remi-
niscent of a speakeasy, the Wild Swann restaurant
in the basement of the boutique hotel that occupies
it now boasts a craft cocktail program and excellent
Bourbon list.

**BUZZARD'S ROOST WHISKEY
ROW EXPERIENCE**
624 West Main Street
BuzzardsRoostWhiskey.com
This microdistillery features an elegant cocktail bar
and special programming detailing the history and
science of whiskey making, plus a special pairing of
whiskey and chocolate. Buzzard's Roost uniquely
ages its whiskey in combinations of more than 20
customized secondary barrels to develop a variety
of expressions. You can buy some of Buzzard Roost's
limited releases only here.

ART EATABLES

631 West Main Street

ArtEatables.com

A certified Bourbon chocolatier, owner Kelly Ramsey creates signature chocolate truffles for almost every distillery in Kentucky. The shop includes a Bourbon tasting bar, where patrons can sample and purchase the whiskeys used in the confections.

21c MUSEUM HOTEL

700–706 West Main Street

21cMuseumHotels.com/louisville

This hotel also functions as a contemporary art museum with permanent and rotating exhibitions. (The name abbreviates "21st century.") Original artwork decorates the bedrooms and suites, too. The Proof on Main restaurant (page 206) features a Bourbon-inflected menu and an excellent Bourbon list. You can buy the hotel's private barrel selections in the lobby gift shop.

PURSUIT SPIRITS

722 West Main Street

pursuitspirits.com

Founded by Kenny Coleman and Ryan Cecil, who host the *Bourbon Pursuit* podcast, this Whiskey Row attraction provides samples from several barrels of Bourbon and ryes. You can then thieve your choice from its barrel, decant into a bottle, seal, label, and buy it. Cocktail bar and speakeasy, too.

BARDSTOWN BOURBON COMPANY TASTING ROOM

730 West Main Street

BardstownBourbon.com/louisville

On a wall next to the cocktail bar, a wood mosaic QR code will take you to videos of the Bardstown campus (page 171). You can enjoy premium tastings and interactive classes here, but the space mostly consists of a retail shop selling all the company's whiskeys in its extensive portfolio.

LOUISVILLE SLUGGER MUSEUM & FACTORY

800 West Main Street

SluggerMuseum.com

A 120-foot-tall baseball bat leaning against the building identifies the location. You can see the iconic swingers being made here and bats signed by most of the sport's greats. The founder of parent company Hillerich & Bradsby originally made Bourbon barrels, so the Barrels & Billets program gives you a chance to taste and blend your own whiskey. (A billet is the piece of wood that becomes a bat.) Note the proportional baseball embedded in the window of the plate-glass factory next door.

MICHTER'S FORT NELSON DISTILLERY

801 West Main Street

michters.com

See page 89.

FRAZIER HISTORY MUSEUM AND KENTUCKY BOURBON TRAIL WELCOME CENTER

829 West Main Street

FrazierMuseum.org

An entire floor of this museum devoted to Kentucky history includes exhibits about Bourbon, complete with a bar. One display features all the bottles produced in the state, and you can (try to) tally how many you've tried. The ground floor bottle shop sells several rare or vintage whiskeys no longer made. The museum also houses the Kentucky Bourbon Trail Welcome Center, which offers maps, videos, and other handy tools for planning.

KENTUCKY PEERLESS DISTILLING CO.

120 North 10th Street

KentuckyPeerless.com

See page 133.

Recommended Restaurants and Bars

Louisville

In 2009, Louisville Tourism created the Urban Bourbon Trail (UBT) with eight restaurants. As of 2024, that number had grown to 35. Inclusion requires a list of at least 50 Bourbons and the notable use of Bourbon in dishes on the food menu. For a complete, up-to-date list, visit BourbonCountry.com/things-to-do/urban-bourbon-trail. Follow a QR code there to download the Urban Bourbon Trail app. The following list includes some of the most notable among them—designated by the "UBT" acronym—plus establishments with excellent lists that don't meet the food criterion. United Parcel Service designated Louisville one of its world hubs, so even though Derby City anchors the land-locked Bluegrass State, it still offers high-quality seafood. Fresh catches are flown in daily from as far away as Hawaii.

THE BLACK RABBIT

122 Sears Avenue
BlackRabbitLouisville.com
This three-in-one venue— lounge, dining room, speakeasy—offers a very good Bourbon list and expertly crafted cocktails.

BOURBONS BISTRO (UBT)

2255 Frankfort Avenue
BourbonsBistro.com
Louisville's first dedicated Bourbon bar and restaurant opened in 2005. The southern-inspired menu includes an exemplary bread pudding studded with cherries and topped with a Bourbon caramel sauce.

DOC CROW'S SOUTHERN SMOKEHOUSE AND RAW BAR (UBT)

127 West Main Street
DocCrows.com
See page 201. Doc's Bourbon Room, a sister establishment next door, has an equally impressive list and a small plates menu.

HELL OR HIGH WATER (UBT)

112 West Washington Street
HellorHighWaterBar.com
A white globe over the door identifies this speakeasy tucked underneath Whiskey Row that features period decor, cozy private rooms, and a fine Bourbon and cocktails list.

THE LAST REFUGE

600 East Market Street
TheLastRefuge.com
Located in a deconsecrated 19th-century church in NuLu and affiliated with Bob Dylan's Heaven's Door Bourbon—which is building a distillery in Pleasureville, Kentucky—it features a soaring 25-foot wall of whiskeys striving to be the largest collection of Bourbon anywhere.

NEAT BOURBON BAR & BOTTLE SHOP (UBT)

1139 Bardstown Road
NeatBottleBar.com
Explore a long list of dusties by the taste or bottle.

NOOK & NOWHERE
1149 South Shelby Street
MatsonGilman.com/trouble-bar
Nestled in a circa 1880 building in Shelby Park, this combination bookstore, coffee bar, and Bourbon lounge caters to a diverse clientele. The menu offers outstanding cocktails and a short list of pastries and sandwiches.

NORTH OF BOURBON
935 Goss Avenue
NorthOfBourbon.com
Enjoy Cajun cuisine, excellent cocktails, and a very long Bourbon list in charming booths built to resemble giant Bourbon barrels.

PROOF ON MAIN (UBT)
702 West Main Street
ProofOnMain.com
The restaurant and bar of the 21c Museum Hotel (page 202) boats more than 30 private barrel selections at any given time, outstanding cocktails, and of course modern art.

RED HOG RESTAURANT AND BUTCHER SHOP
2622 Frankfort Avenue
RedHogArtisanMeat.com
Locally sourced gourmet meats anchor the elegant menu, which does seafood equally well. The small café features steampunk decor and outdoor dining. The long Bourbon list includes some high-end pours and curated cocktails.

RIVER HOUSE RESTAURANT & RAW BAR (UBT)
3015 River Road
RiverHouseLouisville.com
Sip excellent Bourbon cocktails, including a smoked Old-Fashioned, in this beautiful location on the Ohio River. The long Bourbon list includes many private selections, and River House has the best fresh oyster list in the city.

WATCH HILL PROPER (UBT)
11201 River Beauty Loop, Prospect
WatchHillProper.com
Located just outside Louisville, this dining destination offers a fine dining menu of small and large plates and more than 2,100 American whiskeys served amid wood-and-leather clubby decor. The Bourbon list constantly grows, and behind the bar, a library ladder gives staff access to a multitiered wall of bottles.

Lexington

BAR ONA
108 Church Street
facebook.com/ona108/
The Art Deco interior could have come straight from a 1930s film, the perfect intimate setting for an extensive cocktail menu and fine Bourbon list.

BELLE'S COCKTAIL HOUSE
156 Market Street
BellesBar.com
Overlooking downtown Lexington, this multilevel bar with a roof deck, exposed brick walls, and deep leather sofas serves expertly crafted and generously portioned cocktails.

THE BLUEGRASS TAVERN
115 Cheapside
TheBluegrassTavern.com
This historic venue with a pressed tin ceiling delights serious Bourbon lovers with an impressive list of more than 900 Bourbons, ryes, and American malts.

BOURBON ON RYE
115 West Main Street
BourbonOnRye.com
The list here includes all the big-name Kentucky brands and lesser-known labels from in and out of state, plus a great selection of international whiskeys.

DISTILLED ON JEFFERSON
157 Jefferson Street
DistilledonJefferson.com
A long whiskey list and carefully curated cocktails anchor the Bourbon program, with the bistro menu served in a warren of comfortable rooms.

ELKHORN TAVERN
1200 Manchester Street
BarrelHouseDistillery.com/elkhorn-tavern
Next door to Barrel House Distillery (page 95), this bar sports Kentucky hunting lodge decor and specializes in cocktails using Barrel House spirits.

HENRY CLAY'S PUBLIC HOUSE
112 North Upper Street
This 1805 building once served as statesman Henry Clay's office and townhouse. It offers an excellent list of premium Bourbons, many rare or allocated.

OBC KITCHEN
3373 Tates Creek Road
OBCKitchen.com
The initials stand for Old Bourbon Country, and the list of more than 1,000 Bourbons, ryes, American malts, and single-malt Scotches has very few gaps. It does flights, cocktails, and private barrel selections.

Bardstown

BARDSTOWN BOURBON COMPANY
1500 Parkway Drive
BardstownBourbon.com
See page 171. You don't need to take a tour to enjoy the bar and restaurant.

TALBOTT TAVERN
107 West Stephen Foster Avenue
TalbottTavern.com
On the central square, this 18th-century coaching inn still provides accommodation, and the southern-inflected restaurant has a dedicated Bourbon bar.

Covington / Newport

OLD KENTUCKY BOURBON BAR
629 Main Street, Covington
OldKYBourbonBar.com
The list features more than 700 Bourbons and 200 American whiskeys, many available by the bottle, including the bar's private barrel selections. It has an excellent selection of dusties, too.

PROHIBITION BOURBON BAR
530 Washington Avenue, Newport
NewberryBrosCoffee.com
In a room adjacent to a locally owned coffee house, this welcoming, neighborly speakeasy dispenses hundreds of selections, including many premium and hard-to-find pours.

Frankfort

BOURBON ON MAIN
103 West Main Street
BourbonOnMain.com
This attractive destination serves hundreds of Bourbons—many of them limited releases—specialty cocktails, and good bar food.

CAPITAL CELLARS
227 West Broadway Street
CapitalCellars.com
If you know a wine drinker who doesn't know or love Bourbon, come here for excellent selections of whiskey and wine, plus a tasting bar for both.

SERAFINI RESTAURANT & BAR
243 West Broadway Street
SerafiniFrankfort.com
Kentucky legislators frequent this establishment for its Bourbon list—with many selections from nearby Buffalo Trace—and cocktails that pair well with the Kentucky-Italian food menu.

Owensboro

THE MILLER HOUSE
301 East 5th Street
TheMillerHouseRestaurant.com
Hundreds of whiskeys line the walls of the Spirits Bar in the basement of this historic house dating from 1905.

Paducah

BARREL & BOND
100 Broadway Street
BarrelandBond.com
At this great place to taste Bourbon history, four tiers of shelves behind the bar include many rare bottles from the 1960s and '70s. It does private barrel selections, too.

THE FREIGHT HOUSE
330 South 3rd Street
FreightHouseFood.com
Award-winning chef Sara Bradley has amassed an enviable Bourbon collection that she offers at this excellent restaurant and bar. Trust the advice of the bartenders.

Annual Events

Kentucky has a variety of Bourbon festivals and conferences that attract people from around the country and the world, from high-end, highly curated affairs to music for the masses. Nearly all the events have a culinary component. For precise details, including dates and prices, visit the websites. Many of the more exclusive activities sell out quickly, so register early when possible, particularly for September, which is National Bourbon Heritage Month.

February

BOURBON CLASSIC, LOUISVILLE

BourbonClassic.com

Sponsored by the *Bourbon Review* magazine, the Classic first took place in 2013. The Cocktail & Culinary Challenge pairs regional chefs and bartenders, with dishes and drinks judged by an expert panel and by attendees. Bourbon University features whiskey education sessions. Bourbon tastings include some hard-to-find brands, and, yes, you may find Pappy Van Winkle among them.

May

BBQ & BARRELS, OWENSBORO

bbqandbarrels.com

Owensboro gave rise to Western Kentucky–style barbecue—mutton and burgoo—and hosts the Bluegrass Music Hall of Fame & Museum. In this latest iteration of a long-standing barbecue festival, food, music, and Bourbon enjoy equal billing.

August

THE BOURBON WOMEN SIPOSIUM, LOUISVILLE

Bourbonwomen.org/siposium

The annual conference of the Bourbon Women Association—based in Kentucky, with nearly 20 branches throughout America—features premium tastings, behind-the-scene tours, and workshops including food pairings, cocktail classes, the science of barrel chemistry, and insider accounts of woman-owned brands. Panel discussions with industry leaders cover such topics as educational opportunities for aspiring whiskey professionals.

September

KENTUCKY BOURBON FESTIVAL, BARDSTOWN

kyBourbonfestival.com

At the longest-running Bourbon festival in America, which lasts for five days, distilleries large and small offer tastings and sell their whiskeys on the Great Lawn. Other tents and booths present a variety of specialty Kentucky foods and books related to Kentucky and Bourbon. Events with master distillers include blending workshops, cocktail classes, and more tastings. In the barrel relay, teams of distillery warehouse staff roll barrels around a track for accuracy and speed.

▲ A Bourbon Women SIPosium tasting class

BOURBON & BEYOND, LOUISVILLE

Bourbonandbeyond.com

Billed as "the world's largest" Bourbon and music festival, the four-day event attracts more than 140,000 fans, who enjoy more than 60 acts performing rock and roll, blues, country, and more. Headliners have included Jon Batiste, Brandi Carlile, Duran Duran, Bruno Mars, Stevie Nicks, Pearl Jam, and Sting. Chefs from around the country offer tastings, and the Big Bourbon Bar serves the whiskeys.

LOUDER THAN LIFE, LOUISVILLE

louderthanlifefestival.com

Also a Danny Wimmer Production, like Bourbon & Beyond, the largest hard-rock / heavy-metal fest anywhere boasts similar attendance numbers, its own Big Bourbon Bar, and chef-prepared food. Foo Fighters, Green Day, Megadeath, Metallica, Queens of the Stone Age, Tool, and hundreds of other performers have taken to the stages for the four-day experience.

October

BOURBON ON THE BANKS, FRANKFORT

Bourbononthebanks.org

On the Friday night before the main event, a VIP reception (separate ticket) auctions many rare Bourbons to benefit the Kentucky Historical Society. For the Saturday afternoon session, more than 60 distilleries set up booths lining the pathway along the Kentucky River. Past activities have included a pub stroll, Bourbon and food pairing, and a Saturday night after-party.

Distillery Checklist

- ☐ Augusta Distillery
- ☐ Bardstown Bourbon Company
- ☐ Barrel House Distilling Company
- ☐ Bluegrass Distillers
- ☐ Boone County Distilling Company
- ☐ Buffalo Trace Distillery
- ☐ Bulleit Distilling Company
- ☐ Casey Jones Distillery
- ☐ Castle & Key Distillery
- ☐ Dueling Grounds Distillery
- ☐ Four Roses Distillery
- ☐ Green River Distilling Company
- ☐ Heaven Hill Distillery
- ☐ James B. Beam Distilling Company
- ☐ James E. Pepper Distilling Company
- ☐ Jeptha Creed Distillery
- ☐ Kentucky Artisan Distillery
- ☐ Kentucky Peerless Distilling Company
- ☐ Limestone Branch Distillery
- ☐ Log Still Distillery
- ☐ Louisville Distilling Company
- ☐ Lux Row Distillers
- ☐ Maker's Mark Distillery
- ☐ MB Roland Distillery
- ☐ Michter's Distillery
- ☐ Neeley Family Distillery
- ☐ New Riff Distilling
- ☐ Old Forester Distilling Company
- ☐ Old Pogue Distillery
- ☐ Preservation Distillery
- ☐ Rabbit Hole Distillery
- ☐ Second Sight Spirits
- ☐ Stitzel-Weller Distillery
- ☐ Town Branch Distillery
- ☐ Wilderness Trail
- ☐ Wild Turkey Distilling Company
- ☐ Willet Distillery
- ☐ Woodford Reserve Distillery

ACKNOWLEDGMENTS

Thanks to the remarkable growth of the Kentucky Bourbon industry in the last two decades, I had a lot of territory to cover in this book. That would have been impossible without the cooperation of so many people in and associated with the industry. From generously granting me their time in interviews and answering questions to helping arrange those interviews and gathering photos, they were always willing and eager to help, to an individual.

The Kentucky Distillers' Association provided a wealth of information on the economic importance of Bourbon to the state. Eric Gregory and Allison Delande gave me contacts, and Mandy Ryan saved my sanity by giving me access to the KDA's photo files of member distilleries and contact information for permission to use them. Peggy Stevens graciously took time to explain the origins of the KDA's Kentucky Bourbon Trail.

Others who helped me with the content in many ways include Owen Martin, Lori Mattingly, Dee Ford, and Collis Hillebrand (Angel's Envy); Ryan Edwards, Lance Bates, and Alex Castle (Augusta Distillery); Dinah Bird (Baker-Bird Winery and B. Bird Distillery); Dan Callaway and Holly Weyler (Bardstown Bourbon Company); Jake and Jeff Wiseman (Barrel House Distilling Company); Maggie Young (Bluegrass Distillers); Jack Wells (Boone County Distilling Company); Chris Morris, Elizabeth McCall, Melissa Rift, Chris Poynter, and Tracy Frederick (Brown-Forman Corp.); Freddie Johnson, Matt Higgins, and Nick Laracuente (Buffalo Trace Distillery); Amy Dunn and Courtney King (Bulleit Distilling Company); Liz Barrett (Buzzard's Roost); Cody Turner (Casey Jones Distillery); Kelsey Ruddell and Kassidy Price (Castle & Key Distillery); Marc Dottore (Dueling Grounds Distillery); Brent Elliott, Jill Pendygraft, and Ellen Redmon (Four Roses Distillery); and Carlyn Wells and Holly Weyler (Green River Distillery).

Additional help came from Max Shapira, Conor O'Driscoll, Sydney Jones, Lynn House, George Harrison, Kaitlynn West, Lauren Cherry Newcomb, and Sarah Dutton (Heaven Hill Distillery); Fred Noe, Freddie Noe, Linda Hayes, Chris Hood, and Jake Lewellen at BourbonLens.com (James B. Beam Distillery Co.); Amir Peay and Tylar Culver (James E. Pepper Distilling Company); Andrew Pillitteri (Jeptha Creed Distillery); Jade Peterson, Trey Zoeller, Jeremy Dever, Richard Burks, and Angela Bosco (Kentucky Artisan Distillery); Corky Taylor, John Wadell, Cadie Tucker, and Christina Vassallo (Kentucky Peerless Distilling Company); Landon Foster (Limestone Branch Distillery and Lux Row Distillers); Lynne Dant, Charles Dant, Wally Dant, Lindsey Overstreet, and Michael Moeller (Log Still Distillery); Bill Samuels Jr., Rob Samuels, Amanda Humphries and Star, Bob Lauder, Alison Brotzge-Elder, and Kim Ries (Maker's Mark Distillery); and Paul Tomaszewski (MB Roland Distillery).

Helpful cooperation also came from Joe Magliocco, Andrea Wilson, Vicky Fugitte, and Tess Driscoll (Michter's Distillery); Royce Neeley (Neeley Family Distillery); Hannah Lowen and Mollie Lewis (New Riff Distilling); John Pogue (Old Pogue Distillery); Marci Palatella and Shelby Nash (Preservation Distillery); Kaveh Zamanian, Jenna Pallecone, Mason Vowels, Justin Pakdaman, and Madison Graça (Rabbit Hole Distillery); Carus Waggoner (Second Sight Distillery); Angie Buchanan (Stitzel-Weller Distillery); Dave Bob Gaspar and Cheree Redmond (Town Branch Distillery); Jimmy Russell, Eddie Russell, Bruce Russell, Brook Losse, Margaret Bridge, and Lily Newman (Wild Turkey Distillery); Pat Heist and Margaret Bridge (Wilderness Trail Distillery); and Drew Kulsveen and Brittany Allison (Willett Distillery).

More help came from Laura Sutton, who helped

me scout Lexington Bourbon bars; John Johnson of the Wine Rack in Louisville; Tommy Craggs of Watch Hill Proper; Bourbon historian Michael Veach; and photographer Pam Spaulding, who was a very good sport about taking my author photo.

Sincerest thanks to Julian Van Winkle III for writing the thoughtful and lovely foreword to this book. It is an honor. Many thanks to my agent, Londa Kon-ner, for connecting me to the publisher. James Jayo of Countryman Press made this book what it is with his elegant editing. The best author-editor relationship is a partnership, and I was very lucky to enjoy that here.

Finally, a huge thanks to my family—Joanna, Gervase, Winston, Franky, and Jack—for their love and support during the months of traveling, reporting, and writing.

GLOSSARY

ABV: Alcohol by volume, expressed as a percentage and required by law to appear on labels.

Angel's share: The liquid that evaporates from aging barrels. About 7 to 10 percent of total volume evaporates the first year and 3 to 4 percent per year after.

Backset: Liquid from previously fermented mash saved and added, or set back, into a new batch of fermenting mash. Called the sour-mash method, the overall process helps ensure consistency and helps prevent bacteria from tainting fermentation.

Barrel proof: Whiskey bottled directly from the barrel, with no (distilled) water added.

Beer still: Equipment used for the first distillation of **distiller's beer** to produce **low wine**.

Bottled-in-Bond (a.k.a. bonded) Bourbon: An early form of quality control, this designation denotes any American whiskey made at one distillery in one distilling season (January to June or July to December), aged for at least four years in a government-bonded warehouse overseen by a federal gauging agent, and bottled at 50 percent **ABV** (100 **proof**).

Cask strength: See **barrel proof**.

Charring: Directly firing the interior of a barrel for between 15 and 55 seconds to blacken and crack the wood. This process eases the movement of whiskey into the wood and imparts darker flavor notes in the finished product. The char layer also helps filter off flavors.

Contract-distilling: When one distillery, usually larger, produces whiskey for a client, usually smaller.

Cooper: A barrel maker. A cooper works in a cooperage.

Distiller's beer: Liquid strained from fermented mash for distillation. It typically contains about 20 percent **ABV** (40 **proof**).

Doubler: A copper still, usually smaller than a **beer still**, which distills **low wines** into **new-make whiskey**.

Dusties: Vintage or otherwise hard-to-find bottles.

Expressions: Different versions of a whiskey brand, which can vary in age and/or proof, for example: Weller Special Reserve, Weller 12 Year, and Weller Antique.

Fermenter (also fermentation tank): The vessel in which **yeast** digests extracted sugars in cooked mash to produce alcohol. Older fermenters may consist of cypress; newer ones, usually stainless steel.

Low wine: The first distillation, created from running **distiller's beer** through a **doubler**.

Malt: The process of moistening barley, sprouting it, and drying it to produce enzymes that convert mash starches into sugar that **yeast** transforms into alcohol.

Mash bill: The proportional recipe of grains for a whiskey. By law, Bourbon must contain at least 51 percent corn.

New-make whiskey: Unaged whiskey, fresh off the still, colloquially called **moonshine** (but not actually moonshine, since taxes are paid on it), especially when flavored to help mask the high **ABV**.

Non-chill filtered: In chill filtration, cooling the whiskey allows for easy removal of esters, fatty acids, proteins, and other substances that can cause cloudiness at low temperatures, either in storage or when adding cold water or ice. Non-chill filtering retains more flavors from distillation and aging.

Prohibition: "Better than no liquor at all" —Will Rogers

Proof: Alcohol content expressed as double the **abv**. At roughly 100 proof (50 percent ABV), a liquid can maintain combustion.

Red layer: **Toasting** or **charring** a barrel forms this layer of caramelized wood sugars that imparts all the color and 70 percent or more of the flavor to the finished whiskey.

Rickhouse (also rackhouse): A warehouse in which spirits age. In 1879, Frederick Stitzel received a patent for a lattice design allowing air to circulate around the barrels.

Single barrel: All bottles of a given **expression** come from one barrel, which, if bottled at **barrel proof**, can yield about 180 bottles, depending on how long the barrel has aged. (See **angel's share**.) Adding distilled water lowers the proof and increases the bottle yield.

Small batch: No legal definition. The phrase can mean two barrels or 200, depending on a distillery's production volume.

Sour mash: See **backset**.

Sourced: Spirits sold by but not made by a given distiller, which obtained them from elsewhere, either from **contract-distilling** or buying existing finished product.

Staves: Slender pieces of wood that, when inserted into aging whiskey, add flavor.

Straight Bourbon: Aged at least two years.

Sweet mash: Starting each fermentation anew, not using **backset**.

Thieve: To extract small amounts of whiskey from a barrel for quality control or other sampling.

Toasting: Slow-cooking the interior of a barrel with indirect heat that caramelizes sugars in the wood; in contrast to **charring** by direct flame.

Wheated: Whiskey that uses wheat in its **mash bill** in place of or in addition to rye.

Yeast: Single-celled fungi (typically *Saccharomyces cerevisiae*). Sugar + yeast = ethyl alcohol + esters + carbon dioxide. The yeast strain has a strong effect on the final flavor of a whiskey.

FURTHER READING

Berra, Tim. *Bourbon: What the Educated Drinker Should Know*. Morley, MO: Acclaim Press, 2019.

Bryson, Lew. *Tasting Whiskey: An Insider's Guide to the Unique Pleasures of the World's Finest Spirits*. North Adams, MA: Storey Publishing, 2014.

_____. *Whiskey Master Class: The Ultimate Guide to Understanding Scotch, Bourbon, Rye, and More*. Beverly, MA: Harvard Common Press, 2020.

Campbell, Sally Van Winkle. *But Always Fine Bourbon: Pappy Van Winkle and the Story of Old Fitzgerald*. Louisville: Limestone Lane Press, 1999.

Carlson, Carla. Barrel Strength Bourbon: The Explosive Growth of America's Whiskey. Birmingham, AL: Clerisy Press, 2017.

Carson, Gerald. *The Social History of Bourbon*. Foreword by Michael Veach. 1963. Reprint, Lexington: University Press of Kentucky, 2010.

Cecil, Sam K. *The Evolution of the Bourbon Whiskey Industry in Kentucky*. Paducah, KY: Turner Publishing, 1999.

Cowdery, Charles K. *Bourbon, Straight: The Uncut and Unfiltered Story of American Whiskey*. Chicago: Made & Bottled in Kentucky, 2004.

Crowgey, Henry G. *Kentucky Bourbon: The Early Years of Whiskeymaking*. 1971. Reprint, Lexington: University Press of Kentucky, 2008.

Haara, Brian. *Bourbon Justice: How Whiskey Law Shaped America*. Lincoln, NB: Potomac Books, 2018.

Jennings, David. *American Spirit: Wild Turkey Bourbon from Ripy to Russell*. Herdon, VA: Mascot Books, 2020.

Lee, Edward. *Bourbon Land: A Spirited Love Letter to My Old Kentucky Whiskey with 50 Recipes*. New York: Artisan Books, 2024.

Minnick, Fred. *Bourbon: The Rise, Fall, and Rebirth of an American Whiskey*. Minneapolis, MN: Voyageur Press, 2016.

_____. *Bourbon Curious: A Simple Tasting Guide for the Savvy Drinker*, 2nd ed. Minneapolis, MN: Zenith Press, 2019.

_____. *Whiskey Women: The Untold Story of How Women Saved Bourbon, Scotch, and Irish Whiskey*. Lincoln, NB: Potomac Books, 2013.

Mitenbuler, Reid. Bourbon Empire: The Past and Future of America's Whiskey. New York: Viking Penguin, 2015.

Offringa, Hans. *A Field Guide to Whisky: An Expert Compendium to Take Your Passion and Knowledge to the Next Level*. New York: Artisan Books, 2017

Pacult, F. Paul. *American Still Life: The Jim Beam Story and the Making of the World's #1 Bourbon*. Hoboken, NJ: Wiley, 2003.

Regan, Gary, and Mardee Haidin Regan. *The Book of Bourbon and Other Fine American Whiskies*. Shelburne, VT: Chapters Publishing, 1995.

Risen, Clay. *American Whiskey, Bourbon, and Rye,* 2nd ed. New York: Sterling Epicure, 2015.

_____. *Bourbon: The Story of Kentucky Whiskey*. New York: Ten Speed Press, 2021.

Taylor, Richard. *The Great Crossing: A Historic Journey to Buffalo Trace Distillery*. Frankfort: Buffalo Trace Distillery, 2002.

Thompson, Wright. *Pappyland: A Story of Family, Fine Bourbon, and the Things That Last*. New York: Penguin Press, 2020.

Veach, Michael. *Kentucky Bourbon Whiskey: An American Heritage*. Lexington: University Press of Kentucky, 2013.

Young, Al. *Four Roses: The Return of a Whiskey Legend*. Louisville: Butler Books, 2010.

Zoeller, Chester. *Bourbon in Kentucky: A History and Directory of Distilleries in Kentucky*. Louisville: Butler Books, 2009.

IMAGE CREDITS

Augusta Distillery: 178, 179, 180 (both), 181 (both)

Avalon Spirits, Inc.: 87 (left)

Bardstown Bourbon Co./Green River Distilling Co.: 16 (both), 17 (both), 18 (all), 170 (both), 171, 173 (all)

Barrel House Distilling Company: 94, 95 (both)

Bluegrass Distillers: 114, 115, 116–117

Boone County Distilling Company: 162, 163, 164–165, 165

Buffalo Trace Distillery: xx–1, 2, 3, 4 (all), 6 (all), 7, 191

Burks Spring, Kentucky Artisan Distillery: 87 (bottom right)

Campari Group for Wilderness Trail Distillery: 138, 139, 140 (both), 141 (both), 142–143

Casey Jones Distillery: 144, 145, 146, 147 (bottom)

Castle & Key Distillery: 148 (both), 149, 150 (both)

Chatham Imports: 88, 89, 90 (both), 91 (all), 92

Diageo North America, Inc.: 70, 71, 72, 73 (all)

Doe-Anderson on behalf of Maker's Mark: xi, 60, 61, 62, 63 (both), 64, 65, 66 (both), 67, 68, 69 (all), 209, 216, 222

Dueling Grounds Distillery: 152, 153, 154, 155 (all)

Four Roses Distillery LLC: 22 (both), 23, 24, 25, 196–197

Getty Images / koya79: v

Glencairn Crystal: xvii

Heaven Hill Brands: 44, 45, 46, 47, 49 (all), 50, 51

iStock/6381380: xv

iStock/agshotime: 147 (top)

iStock/Althom: 34, 36–37, 42 to 43, 204

iStock/DanBrandenburg: xii

iStock/karenfoleyphotography: xvi, 20, 221

iStock/littleny: 188, 190

iStock/lucentius: 41

iStock/Try Media: xix

Jake Lewellen/BourbonLens.com: 38, 40 (top)

James Pepper Distilling Co.: 96, 97, 98 (all), 99 (both)

Jefferson's Bourbon: 84, 85, 86, 87 (top right)

Jeptha Creed Distillery: 174, 175, 176, 177 (both)

Joanna Goldstein: 40 (bottom)

Julian Van Winkle III: viii

Kentucky Peerless Distilling Co.: ii–iii, 132, 134, 135 (both), 136–137, 203

Kriech-Higdon Photography for Bourbon Classic: 210, 213

Lexington Brewing & Distilling Company: 128, 129, 130, 131 (all)

Log Still Distillery: 192 (all), 193, 194, 195 (both)

Louisville Distilling Company/Angel's Envy: 104, 105, 106 (both), 107, 108–109, 198

Lux Row Distillers/Limestone Branch Distillers: 110, 111, 112 (both), 113 (both), 182, 183 (both), 184 (both), 185 (all), 186–187

MB Roland Distillery: 100, 101, 102 (both), 103 (all)

Michael Borop: vi, 199

Neeley Family Distillery: 166, 167, 168 (both), 169 (both)

New Riff Distilling: 158 (both), 159, 160 (both), 161

Old Forester Distillery: 8, 9, 10–11, 12, 13, 14 (all), 15

Old Pogue Distillery: 118, 119, 120 (both), 121

public domain: 151

Rabbit Hole Distillery: 122, 123, 124, 125 (all), 126–127

Second Sight Spirits: 156, 157 (both)

Stitzel-Weller: 52, 53, 54 (both), 55 (all)

Susan Reigler: 39

Wild Turkey Distillery: 26, 27, 28, 29, 30, 31 (all), 32–33

Willett Distillery: 56, 57 (both), 58, 59 (all)

Woodford Reserve Distillery: 74, 76, 77, 78, 79, 80 (both), 81, 82–83, 214

Zach Sinclair / Grizzly Media: 19, 200, 212

INDEX

Page numbers in **bold** indicate illustrations.